'Seneca once said, "Begin at once t[...]
a separate life." Leaders interested in "being" rather than merely "doing" would do well to pay attention to this book. By practising mindfulness, they will become more awake to what life is putting in front, rather than being caught up in ruminating about the past or believing that happiness lies in being some place else.'
Manfred F. R. Kets de Vries, Distinguished Clinical Professor of Leadership Development and Organizational Change, INSEAD

'Being "present" in leadership, rather than just "doing" it, can make profound differences in how leaders are experienced and their impact. A blend of science and practical ideas, Amanda Sinclair's wonderful new book provides a refreshing account of mindfulness and its relevance to leaders of organizations and communities. I loved it.'
Donna Ladkin, Professor of Leadership and Ethics, Plymouth University, UK

'Sinclair takes us on a journey of leadership based on mindful principles which hold out great hope that leaders can live more purposeful, healthful and joyful lives along with those they lead. Sinclair leaves us with a lovely thought: by being mindful, leaders can be open to others as well as themselves, create caring and compassionate environments and speak truthfully while being strong, courageous, creative and effective in both the routine and sometimes very difficult contexts in which they lead.'
Alan Guskin, Distinguished University Professor, PhD Program in Leadership and Change, University President Emeritus, Antioch University

'*Leading Mindfully* is an engaging and accessible guide to help us all be purposeful leaders content in our own being and as a consequence more effective. It is for all people whose work involves influencing what people think or do—teachers, community leaders, health professionals, as well as "bosses".'
Diane Grady AM, Independent Director of public company and not for profit boards, including Macquarie Group, McKinsey & Co's Senior Advisory Board and The Centre for Ethical Leadership

'It is quite a rare thing for an author to be able to combine academic rigour, practical experience and wisdom. Amanda Sinclair does that beautifully in her valuable and insightful book, *Leading Mindfully*. Those who lead in community, corporate and political circles need to read this book—now!'
Associate Professor Craig Hassed, Monash University

Amanda Sinclair is an author and teacher in leadership, change, ethics and diversity. A Professorial Fellow at the Melbourne Business School, she has written many articles and books on leadership including: *Doing Leadership Differently* and *Leadership for the Disillusioned*. She consults to organisations and senior management teams, coaches individuals and also teaches yoga and meditation.

LEADING MINDFULLY

How to focus on what
matters, influence for good,
and enjoy leadership more

AMANDA SINCLAIR

ALLEN&UNWIN
SYDNEY·MELBOURNE·AUCKLAND·LONDON

First published in 2016

Allen & Unwin
83 Alexander Street
Crows Nest NSW 2065
Australia
Phone: (61 2) 8425 0100
Email: info@allenandunwin.com
Web: www.allenandunwin.com

Cataloguing-in-Publication details are available
from the National Library of Australia
www.trove.nla.gov.au

ISBN 978 1 92526 704 4

Internal design Alissa Dinallo
Set in 12/16 pt Minion by Midland Typesetters
Printed and bound in Australia by Griffin Press

10 9 8 7 6 5 4 3 2 1

CONTENTS

INTRODUCTION

Thank you for considering this book and opening this page. As you begin reading, drop your shoulders away from your ears. Let your jaw soften, then mouth, tongue, right down to the roots of your teeth, relax. Take your attention now to any sounds that surround you. They may be traffic or voices, domestic or office sounds. Attend to all the different sounds without puzzling about what they are or why they are there. This is likely an experience of mindfulness.

Already some of you—those who are persevering and haven't discarded the book in irritation—may be thinking, 'What's this about? I haven't got time for this!' These declamations to oneself are simply thoughts. We all have them. Even the Dalai Lama says he has lots of thoughts. He just doesn't worry about them. Mindfulness is the very simple act of choosing to be present and aware in the moment, observing thoughts rather than getting caught up with them.

I have written this book because my experience tells me that mindfulness and the capacity to be mindful is very valuable to leaders. While there are a lot of wonderful books on mindfulness, there are few that explore how mindfulness can be part of day-to-day leadership. Bringing mindfulness to influencing and leading means making a commitment to valuing people and what is unfolding in the present moment. Leading mindfully thus encourages us to bring attention to who and what is here with us now, rather than being absorbed in the usual leadership fare of striving towards future goals. In this book I describe my experiences in a range contexts over the last decade of working with colleagues and leaders to bring mindfulness into their leadership.

In my own life, learning—over time and often belatedly—to be mindful has helped me to do leadership differently. It has helped me be happier and less driven in my work and life. I think it has also helped me be more effective in helping others—students, people I coach, work with and alongside—find more pleasure and less stress in what they do. This is work I am passionate about. I want people to find ways to do their leadership work that are significant and impactful in achieving good ends. But I equally want them to do so without killing themselves, physically or psychically. Ideally I'd like to encourage people to find pleasure, optimism, sensuality and love, in leading. This is what this book is about.

Speaking about killing oneself—I know a bit about this. Some years ago I had a stress-induced heart attack, a Takasubo cardiomyopathy, which occurs when a huge hit of adrenalin floods the heart, causing it to dilate and stop. I was teaching an executive group at the time. It became hard to breathe. There was a tightness in my chest. My head was saying 'I can keep going' but my heart, quite clearly, was saying 'STOP!' In the ambulance on the way to the hospital, I thought I might not get to meet my daughter's first baby—and my first grandchild—who was due to be born later that year.

This was just one of a series of those moments that life shoved in my face and said, 'Pay attention to what you are doing! Life is not a "To Do" list to be got through!' Neither is leadership about getting through the work. Learning about mindfulness has helped me notice my tendency to drive myself and defer life—'I'll just get through these next six months/this next project and then life will be better.' It has helped me to pause and relish good things happening right under my nose. I have been encouraged to see and make choices about my life and habits which I hadn't seen before.

Importantly, this has not led me into retreat or a cave (though the idea is sometimes attractive!). It has not prompted me to give up my own leadership work but to do it very differently. One of the common misconceptions which I address in this book is that mindfulness is for those of us lucky enough to have the time, discipline and personal arrangements to allow retreat from the frantic material world into deep spiritual reflection. In contrast, and in my experience, cultivating everyday mindfulness is exactly suited to the demands of leadership.

HOW MIGHT MINDFULNESS HELP LEADERS?

As will be already evident, *Leading Mindfully* has emerged partially out of my own efforts to 'be' more and 'do' less in my own leadership work. Often in my own career, I have found myself very busy with, and sometimes exhausted by, *doing* things that are not very important: endless meetings, hours on emails and half-baked exchanges that don't help or change anything much except depleting energies. Although I have blamed institutions and people for imposing these priorities on me, the truth of course is that I have colluded in creating them. In almost all cases, we can choose where and how we place our efforts. At a real and foundational level, then, mindfulness can help leaders make decisions about their energies and where they put them.

Further, though, and potentially radically, how and who you are *being* in leadership may be more important than what you do. This idea is counter to almost all other approaches to leadership which tell us that it is actions—'deeds not words', to quote that frequent school motto—that count. The mark of leadership in conventional accounts is goals achieved, programs implemented, buildings built, change orchestrated. While such outcomes are undeniably important, increasing bodies of evidence, as well as my own observations, indicate that effective leaders find ways to be: to be present to the people around them and the challenges and opportunities of that moment. How leaders are *being* matters just as much in a crisis, when the right decisions and actions need to be taken quickly, as it does in spontaneous exchanges—for example, a hallway conversation with a colleague—and in more reflective moments—such as the way we can silently support someone to speak up or draw attention to something that matters to them.

Growing out of many experiences of teaching and working with managers and leaders, I have been struck by how much difference the quality of how leaders are *being* makes to others. It is often the *being* rather than the *doing* that is inspiring and empowering, that frees others to be bold, to do new and different things, that invites them to be honest and talk about what matters to them. This book charts my journey working with and observing people experimenting with ways of being present and mindful in their leadership work.

WHAT'S MINDFULNESS, AND WHAT'S MINDFULNESS IN A LEADERSHIP CONTEXT?

Mindfulness is a way of being which values awareness of whatever is unfolding in the present moment. The first accounts of mindfulness date back to the Buddha's writings more than two thousand years ago. Still, today, the purest and simplest accounts of what it is like to be mindful come from Buddhist writers and scholars such as the Dalai Lama and the Vietnamese monk Thich Nhat Hanh. What they tell us is that mindfulness involves being awake to what life is putting in front of us, rather than being caught up in ruminating about the past or believing that happiness lies in being 'someplace else'.

A widely used contemporary definition of mindfulness comes from a pioneer in clinical applications of mindfulness, Jon Kabat-Zinn, who describes it as paying attention, on purpose, in the present moment, without judgement.[1] Even simpler is Thich Nhat Hanh's notion of mindfulness as present moment awareness. Although people often ask for a lasting and all-purpose definition of mindfulness, my own experience is that it's not much use. Searching for definition keeps us in the intellectual, appraising realm where we are saying, 'Yes, that's not bad, but what does this bit mean and I'm not sure I will buy that bit . . .' and so on.

More useful in helping people grasp the *experience*, as well as idea, of mindfulness in the day-to-day of lives and work is Kabat-Zinn's summary of some of the mindfulness 'lessons' people are encouraged to explore in the Massachusetts Stress Reduction Clinics he founded in Boston:

> Learning how to suspend all your doing and shift over to *a being mode,* how to make time for yourself, how to slow down and nurture calmness and self-acceptance in yourself, learning to observe what your mind is up to from moment to moment, how to watch your thoughts and let go of them without getting caught up by them and driven by them, how to make room for new ways of seeing old problems and for perceiving the interconnectedness of things . . .[2]

Richard Searle, my long-time friend and colleague on the mindful leadership journey, suggests a simple starting point of understanding mindfulness as attention plus intention.

Relatedly, wise scholars of mindfulness point out that contemporary definitions of mindfulness are a product of this society's current preoccupations and malaises. For example, academics Ronald Purser and Joseph Milillo argue that original Buddhist conceptions placed far more importance on 'the why'—the reasons for, and our intentions in, undertaking mindfulness, which was to relieve suffering and practise compassion. One can even apply mindfulness to letting go of the search for a final definition. It may be just one more thought.

The last two or three decades have seen widespread adoption and research of more limited notions of mindfulness in clinical settings: to help people cope with depression and pain, among other conditions. Psychologist Ellen Langer was a pioneer in exploring the benefits of mindfulness in old age, documenting that regular mindful practices helped delay and reverse mental and physical symptoms of ageing. In her work Langer adopts a specific definition of mindfulness as the cognitive capacities to categorise familiar stimuli in new ways and to elaborate new categories of thought.

This book focuses on the application of mindfulness in work environments and in leadership—an area that has been much less widely documented than medical settings. There are many profound books on mindfulness—some of which I will draw upon in this book—but there are few on practising mindfulness in leadership.[3] Over the last decade I have worked with colleagues in this space, introducing and exploring ideas and practices of mindfulness with managers and leaders from diverse sectors and organisations. This book records some of those experiences, documenting the kinds of challenges faced and how mindfulness changes the way leaders see and work with those challenges. The questions guiding us in our research and our programs is how might mindfulness be incorporated into leadership, to reduce suffering and make organisations and workplaces fulfilling and enjoyable places to be.

Research studies provide increasing amounts of evidence about how mindful practices change us. For example, participating in eight-week courses in mindfulness meditation improves attention and focus, reduces feelings of stress and anxiety, while also improving empathy and compassion for self and others. Each of these three effects of mindfulness—on intention, attention, and emotion or affect—has been subject to further study. Though much research has been undertaken in clinical and laboratory settings, an increasing number of research studies find these outcomes of mindfulness also occur in workplaces and leadership contexts.

Some of this research will be presented in later chapters of the book, along with neuroscientific studies which track the neurological changes—the chemical and physiological changes in neural structures—that accompany mindfulness and mediate its effects on behaviour and attitude. While this is a burgeoning area of research and there is clear evidence that mindfulness does elicit neuroplastic changes, the focus of this book is on the experienced outcomes for leaders and organisations.

What I will suggest is that regular practice of mindfulness gives leaders a different perspective on their world, opening them up to ways of being which are both more focused on what matters and more observant and appreciative of what is there. Paradoxically, becoming more present enables leaders to see reality more clearly and act more purposefully and with less of their own stuff getting in the way. This is one of a number of apparently paradoxical insights which leaders encounter with fresh eyes when exploring mindfulness:

- To open up for change, it is necessary to sometimes stop striving to change things.
- To empower others, stop talking and listen from a different place.
- To go forward with openness and creativity into the future, start with being present to current realities.

- To achieve new things, experiment with doing less and being more.

YET . . . SOME PITFALLS IN PURSUING MINDFULNESS IN LEADERSHIP

The last few years has seen dramatically increased media attention on mindfulness: what it is and isn't, what it can do for organisations and in business. The coming together of leadership with mindfulness is potentially of great benefit. More discussion comes later, especially in Chapter 19 'Being ethical', yet some common pitfalls to be acknowledged at the outset include:

1. Superior thinking or even thinking about thinking is not mindfulness

Mindfulness is not just another category of thinking. Rather, in Buddhism is it sometimes known as 'non-thinking', or awareness that is *not* cluttered by thought. This is an important point because mindfulness has also been used by psychologists to denote a particular form of thinking. Monash University medical academic and pioneer in introducing medical students to mindfulness Craig Hassed has indeed suggested that a condition of excessive thinking may be one of the key causes of stress in contemporary life. He and others have noted that we have an over-reliance on thinking which does us potential harm (more about this in Chapter 2 'Thinking less').

2. Don't get seduced by neuroscience

Mindfulness is not brain plasticity. Although neuroscience and the related cognitive sciences provide fascinating evidence about how and why mindfulness works, changing brain structures are not the same as mindfulness. Much contemporary research equates the mind with the brain, and mindfulness is sometimes treated as an artefact of superior brain functioning. This is a predictable trap for Western-trained researchers with their biases reproducing the dominance of the brain. In many traditional accounts, however, the mind's operations are not located just, or even at all, in the brain. There is evidence that neural-like structures are much more widely distributed in the body—the sources, perhaps, of other kinds of intelligence, such as intuition. At the very least, the mind is not circumscribed by the brain.

3. Mindfulness is not an organisational 'fix'

Leadership as a field is full of fads and fulsome promises. Mindfulness could well be seen as the 'next big thing', the leadership panacea that will 'revolutionise' workplaces (as some of my business peers are wont to enthuse). In Buddhism and other mindful traditions, the advice is be wary of gurus and sales pitches. The only important test is one's own experience. Try it diligently and continue if you notice a positive difference.

4. Leading mindfully is not an invitation to be more self-absorbed

Another pitfall in leadership and potentially in mindfulness is the belief that these practices are all about individual mastery. It is useful to remember that we can't do leadership or mindfulness within this individualistic paradigm. In mindfulness we are just a small part of long, rich and diverse lineages of teachers and practitioners. Similarly, effective leadership is never a solo activity. Leading mindfully is all about how we are with others, about what new and valuable things might happen *through* us, because of how we are being, rather than what we do.

5. You don't have to retreat to a cave to be mindful

A common view of mindfulness is that it is an intensely private process which people need to dedicate time and go 'offline' to do. Drawing a distinction between mindfulness and meditation may be helpful. While the two are deeply interrelated, meditation is a practice of sitting (or walking) in a state of conscious awareness, while mindfulness is bringing a state of awareness to whatever we may be doing. Writers such as Thich Nhat Hanh and contemporary teachers such as Kabat-Zinn emphasise that mindfulness is of limited value if we are not seeking to live it in our relationships with others, our work and everyday lives. And this is why mindfulness has such potential for leadership: because it can be practised in the thick of whatever we are doing or wherever we happen to be. We can be in a team meeting discussion or have a conversation with a colleague with mindfulness. The evidence is that others involved in those moments will notice a difference. They will feel more heard and more held to embark on whatever challenge or opportunity that is before them.

LOOKING IN DIFFERENT PLACES FOR LEADERSHIP—WHO THIS BOOK DRAWS ON AND IS FOR

In my own investigations of leadership—with a focus not just on the doing but the being—I have often been most inspired by leaders operating in areas of public life that lie beyond corporate organisations. It is often in the leadership work of community workers, entrepreneurs, activists, teachers, artists and community organisers that we see leadership practices that promise freedom and change. This leadership is usually happening on the fringes and peripheries of conventional corporate and bureaucratic institutions. It is happening in communities and among volunteers, among people working in creative sectors.

I have been lucky to have been involved in a big research project over the last few years, the aim of which was to map women's leadership over a century of Australian democracy. What this research has revealed is the extensive leadership that has been provided by Australian women—in politics, community and Indigenous affairs and elsewhere—often against intractable institutional obstacles, including people in positions of formal leadership determined to keep those same women silent and powerless. Typically what these women did was not given that leadership label, but their courage, ingenuity and perseverance is proof of the diversity of ways leadership and influence can be exercised to change societies for the good.[4]

The most inspiring leadership is sometimes not even described as that, or given the leadership label by the people doing it. For example, I did some work with correctional officers—prison managers and officers in a state-based corrections organisation. These groups occupy a 'frontline' where leadership is not necessarily being delivered by those in authority. They are enacting (sometimes reluctantly and under dangerous conditions) cultural change, including pushing back on norms, moving the mindset from incarceration to rehabilitation; trying to reduce and reverse corrupting and debilitating mindsets; trying new things for themselves that demand more of them and different things of them. The more they talked about this, the clearer it became that this was leadership of a most demanding kind, and I found them inspiring. But leadership was not a label they gave to the work. However, in the process of working together, I believe it was helpful for them to validate and recognise the leadership *in* their work. It helped support them and give themselves agency to persevere when cynicism or withdrawal would be much easier paths.

So, while 'leadership' may be one of those big words with so much baggage in it that many of us want to distance ourselves from it, I urge you to stay with the possibility that leadership is important, and most of us are involved in it in some way or another. All positive social changes involve leadership by individuals and groups. Even apparently small initiatives can change people's lives in noticeable, beneficial ways. An example I heard recently is of the manager of an aged-care residential home seeing that the residents might enjoy the structure of a book club—the opportunity to read together and discuss certain books rather than doing so alone. Listening to residents aged in their 80s and 90s describe their delight in book club discussions left no doubt that the centre manager's idea, instinct and initiative to make this happen was an example of leadership. Her capacity to follow through, working out ways to overcome or go around the various, inevitable resource and other hurdles put in her way, is demonstrable leadership. She saw herself primarily as simply doing her job. However, as the book club took on its own life, she also became part of it, relishing the intelligence and humour of the residents.

In this book I draw on lots of examples of people who don't think of themselves as exercising leadership. I hope it will be useful and readable for those of you who don't see yourself as leaders: people working in organisations at all levels, in the community, people working for themselves and in small business, parents, carers, volunteers, family members, all of us who have opportunities through our own example or through advice to guide and support others in life. I aim to show that leading mindfully can be a path of enjoyment and pleasure, a process in which you don't have to turn yourself into someone else.

WHY THIS BOOK IS WRITTEN THIS WAY

If any of the above sounds earnest, I hope that the way you experience this book is not. Too many leadership books—and good books with important things to say—are not read. In my view they fall into one of two categories. There are the blockbuster types—'How to be a great CEO like me'. They tell you what you should do but in the end are not helpful because they are simplistic and fail to speak to the doubts, frailty and fears that are often companions as we walk any kind of leadership path.

Alternatively, books on leadership are dense and daunting. A lot of us who write about leadership unfortunately have got a lot to say—too much. So each new book on leadership has to position itself around all that has already been written. Of course, I may just have done that myself. However, I can at least reassure you that I have sought to be mindful in how I have written this, as well as what I am writing about. My intention was to write simply and directly, from my experience and my heart.

Most of the ideas I explore here are not new, though some rarely appear, or are seen to apply, in leadership. This book won't tell you what I, or others, think you should do in leadership. Instead I want to offer a series of 'meditations' on aspects of *being* in leadership.[5] Not designed to be comprehensive or claim to be all you should know, the contents reflect my journey around leadership and mindfulness. Whoever said leadership should be pleasurable, even sensuous, that leading well might include loving those, in some lights, unlikeable colleagues? Well, I am.

While the emphasis is on the more interior aspects of being and being in leadership, this is not a book that asks 'how are we to lead' in an intellectual or philosophical sense. Instead I want to actively avoid equating us and our contribution as leaders with what we accomplish by applying our usual intellectual resources to the challenge. Rather, I invite other parts of you on this journey of exploring aspects of life in leadership: your instincts, your feelings, your memories, your practical wisdom, your hunches about what works and what gets in the way, your breathing and gut, your misgivings, desires and hopes.

The most recent image I have had as I've been writing this book is the one from the movie *Forrest Gump*. The main character, Forrest, played by actor Tom Hanks, says life is like a box of chocolates. I hope this book is a metaphorical box of twenty chocolates: each chapter with different blends of insights, research, examples, anecdotes. Some that hit the spot and others that, at the moment, are less to your taste. You can choose any chapter, and read them in any order. So, I'd like *Leading Mindfully* to be in your bag, by the couch or bed, for you to open it at some page, find something arresting or diverting for the next few moments, before perhaps nodding off into a contented sleep.

A BIT ABOUT MY JOURNEY WITH LEADING MINDFULLY

I came to mindfulness by the route of difficulty and pain—a not uncommon route which is reflected in the first Buddhist noble truth: life is suffering. For me, 1996 was a tough year with my brother's sudden death at 45 and the loss of my grandfather a few months later. I'd lost my dad when I was fourteen, and Pop had become a beacon of humble self-sufficiency and generosity of spirit to all our family. My older brother had tried meditation after my brother died and, following that, I took myself and my mother off to some free classes run by followers of Sri Chinmoy. I found the practice and teacher powerful, bought the tape and got a sense of what might be available. But life got busy in 1997 with the birth of my fourth child, Charlie, and I didn't return to exploring mindfulness until a subsequent crisis—this time career—in 2003.

By that time I'd been a professor for some years, teaching and researching largely in leadership. On the outside, I was successful and influential. Yet inside I felt most painfully that I wasn't providing any leadership myself. I was participating in a punishing academic regime with its norms of sacrificing life to work. The 'leadership' I was part of seemed to be exacerbating suffering, not helping people find satisfaction and meaning in their lives. At a personal level I'd lost connection with what mattered to me as an academic and educator. Caught up with activities that didn't seem to make much difference, I felt 'stuck', distracted and unavailable to my family and friends.

Deciding to resign, I was encouraged by the then dean of the Business School to take leave without pay instead. During the following year, I sat in the garden and got RSI from overuse of the milk frother for lattes with friends. More usefully, I finished training to be a yoga teacher and read widely in yoga and Buddhist philosophy. I learned that the purpose of yoga is to improve one's capacity to understand and restrain the mind's 'modifications', that the body work of yoga is just the gateway. At the end of that wonderful year—the highlight of which was teaching Charlie and his preschool mates yoga—I faced what seemed to be a stark choice. Yoga teacher, or back to being a professor?

Initially, and after completing further meditation teacher training with the Gawler Foundation, my efforts were around introducing yoga and meditation into the environments in which I was working. Increasingly, however, the opportunity seemed to be one of bringing mindfulness into the heart of leadership. I had the feeling—after teaching a lunch-hour yoga class where we had experienced some mindfulness—that this modest interlude was doing more potential good for people than a whole semester of leadership classes.

For me, connecting mindfulness and leadership has meant:

- putting people's well-being and flourishing first and, at the very least, not adding to suffering in what I do and urge others to do
- taking off my armour and allowing myself to be vulnerable
- working with my whole self, my senses, body and heart as much as my head
- letting go of ego stuff like needing the approval of others.

It has meant asking questions such as:

- How can leadership contribute to freeing people?
- How might leaders be helped to be more present to those they are seeking to lead?
- How can leadership reduce suffering and support people to achieve great things but also find peace and fulfilment?

Asking the questions above and seeking to make these changes in myself has evidently looked idealistic and sentimental to some. But it has got easier as I have stopped worrying about others labelling me as 'naïve' or 'touchy-feely'—a move facilitated by the recognition that those fears about how others see you are just the usual workings of ego and not to be given great importance.

I am, and continue to be, a novice in mindfulness. Passing on these experiences about mindfulness in leadership, I hope, will simply open some doorways for you to further reading and exploration with those who are more adept than me.

Neither am I Buddhist, though I have been and continue to be profoundly influenced by Buddhist writers and teachers. I am following the Dalai Lama's advice here, which is to follow an ethical path—whether religious or secular—deriving from our cultural backgrounds, philosophies and educational experiences.

In its three-part structure, the book mirrors my own journey with mindfulness and leadership. Part One is about the mind and rethinking the more recognisable activities that are part of exercising leadership from a mindfulness perspective. It reflects where I, and I think most of us, are encouraged to start out—and sometimes stay—in our education and careers. I was brought up to believe my capacity to think and be smart was critical to success—indeed, it felt, to my very survival. It was my route to recognition. My capacity to think and be smart *was* me.

However, as I describe above, during my career as an academic and academic leader, I started to confront the possibility that my mind and my drive to keep being smart and in control was killing me—it certainly was leading to a great deal of unhappiness as I strove to drive myself harder to achieve, but was disconnected from relationships and the bigger picture of life and what we are here for.

Hence Part Two of the book suggests that paying attention to the body, the senses and the breath, rather than trying to ignore or control them, is a reliable way in to being present and mindful. The start of my journey in mindfulness was with the physical. In desperation and feeling very out of control of my life, I followed the referral of a friend to a yoga class. Initially I just wanted to feel more able to deal with what life was throwing at me. I came out of those first yoga classes feeling strong and, with palpable relief, able to get perspective on my life and work. Undertaking yoga teacher training and starting to meditate introduced me to completely new ways of understanding the mind. It also introduced the radical notion that the purpose of life might be to be happy, that it was not only acceptable but a good objective to care for one's well-being.

Steadily and inexorably, I came to learn that the physical and the senses are precious and important gateways to living differently, with openness, compassion and love. While these ideas and practices seemed eminently worthwhile in my personal life, could they also be relevant to leadership? Part Threee charts my ongoing efforts to learn for myself and explore with others how to lead with an open and warm heart.

PART ONE

LEADERSHIP FOR LIFE

How can we do leadership in a way that is life affirming? How can we subtly shift the day-to-day of our work to influence and support those around us and make those interactions not just effective but even pleasurable and occasionally profound? The 'meditations' or chapters in this first part of the book take some activities that are a familiar part of leading and reconsider how to do them mindfully. Individual chapters cover common tasks such as listening, giving attention and leading discussions or dialogue. But, in each, I invite you to explore and experiment with making small changes in the direction of mindfulness that I suggest can have big impacts.

Each of these activities aimed at enhancing mindfulness are ones that, with colleagues and particularly my good friend Richard Searle, have been introduced to the very diverse groups with whom we've had the opportunity to work over the last decade. This work includes running four-day dedicated Mindful Leadership programs for executives, which we began in 2007; in leadership development programs at Mt Eliza Executive

Education, which Richard co-directed; and with MBA and EMBA students that I teach at Melbourne Business School. We have introduced mindfulness to many leaders and executive teams in diverse sectors and industries, including insurance, banking and engineering companies, senior police and prison officers, academics and Indigenous leaders, school, health and hospital leaders, public sector leaders and those attending women's leadership programs, which I run with another great colleague and friend, Christine Nixon. Mindfulness is also an important part of my work coaching individual leaders. In *Leading Mindfully* I relate some of these experiences and the ideas and practices that leaders find most helpful for the variety of leadership work they are doing.

As can be seen from this list, the development of these mindful approaches in leadership has been a very collaborative one. Throughout this book I refer to many other mindful leaders who have inspired me with their sustained, often quiet, commitment to introducing mindfulness into their own work and contexts. These include David White, Diane Grady, Gordon Cairns and other business leaders who have been running the Sydney Leaders Retreat under the guidance of Sogyal Rinpoche for a decade, medical academic Craig Hassed and his colleagues at Monash University, Melbourne public health academic and advocate Rob Moodie, consultants and authors Martina Sheehan and Susan Pearse who founded Brisbane-based Mind Gardener, doctor and psychiatric specialist Elise Bialylew who created Mindful in May, and Jono Fisher and his colleagues at the Sydney-based Wake Up Project, a community of individuals committed to promoting mindful living and leadership.

So, none of these ideas about leading mindfully are new. Yet I hope that offering them in this way—as simple, practical areas of experimentation for leaders—is useful. Indeed, feedback suggests that being introduced to ways of being mindful, for example, being given the opportunity to try meditation, are valuable—sometimes transforming—for people in their work and broader lives.

One

BEING AS WELL AS DOING IN
LEADERSHIP

What we achieve inwardly will change outer reality.
Plutarch, quoted by J.K. Rowling

Leadership is not a position or a person but a process of influence between individuals and within groups towards valued
outcomes. Thus leadership can be (ands often is) exercised
without formal authority and from all parts of organisations
and groups: from the bottom as well the top, from the edges as
well as the centre.

However, there are many misconceptions about leadership
and what it involves—often created by leadership books! One
misconception is that leadership is what people in authority—the
heads of companies and schools, officials, elected representatives,
members of boards—do. Another is that leadership involves
getting through the work of implementing mandates. A third
is that leadership is about coming up with a 'vision' which will
ensure organisational survival despite intense competition and
turbulence.

Many of these misconceptions are not helpful for those
engaged in leadership. They set the bar too high, they are

unrealistic and punishing, and they often result in well-intentioned capable people feeling like failures because they're not leaders 'out front' or visionaries with a crystal clear view of where everyone should be heading. Because of these misconceptions, valuable leadership work is not recognised because people haven't 'delivered' on infeasible or unhelpful benchmarks; or because the way they do the work doesn't match heroic templates.

Contemporary societies, particularly managerial and organisational domains, put a high value on what people 'do'. Often when I ask groups of students or managers to introduce themselves, I expressly ask them to mention something other than their occupation, role or employer. Despite my explicit request, many self-introductions veer back to job titles and activities: manager, planner, director, financial or marketing executive. Most of us are brought up to collude with the idea that we are our jobs or professions. Actions and occupations define us. They are the way we know who we are. What we do anchors our legitimacy and value in the world.

Leaders are also selected, valued and rewarded for being focused on the future, for projecting a big picture confidently, for what Harvard University leadership scholar Ron Heifetz has called salesmanship. They've often had a focus on future results built into their performance contracts, so every action is undertaken with a view to securing a future state of affairs (market share or dominance, growth targets reached via acquisitions, return on investment and so on).

Yet these views cause problems—for the leaders themselves, for the people working around them, and for their organisations. Leadership in practice is rarely as easy as implementing one's predefined vision by getting others to do things. Nor is it ticking off the items on the board's agenda. There is sometimes a lot of pressure in organisations to see leadership in this way. According to Heifetz and his colleagues, there is a critical distinction here between authority and leadership that many individuals and organisations confuse.[1] Authority is the power that others give you to do what they have determined is important. But getting these things done—especially if they are the things that predecessors or other stakeholders insist must be done—is rarely reliably leadership. Fulfilling at least some expectations may be important, but often the work of leadership involves disrupting, disappointing or changing those expectations.

In the book's introduction I described a couple of periods of my life and career which provided powerful catalysts for me to step back and confront how I was being. These crises left little doubt that I needed to change the way I was doing my own leadership work. My initial—and perhaps a necessary response—was to 'do less and be more'. I cleared my diary of all but the most essential work commitments, I weaned myself off email, only checking every couple of days. I scrutinised all the extra opportunities and invitations that came my way, applying the test of: 'Will I really be able to make a difference to people with this?' If not, I made suggestions about who else might be interested and do a great job. I gave a keynote address with the title 'Doing less and being more in leadership'.

While my own experience is that we sometimes need to radically alter the balance between doing and being, in reality they are not alternatives. Leadership inevitably involves doing. But it is also a trap and for many of us it's the place to go when we are under pressure or working in ambiguity—the doing is more familiar and sometimes seductive than stopping and being in a place that may feel aimless, confronting or way outside one's usual competence.

When I work with leaders and managers, I seek to convey this shift with a table like the one below (see Figure 1: Emphases in traditional versus mindful leadership), contrasting traditional emphases in leadership on doing with some 'being' alternatives.

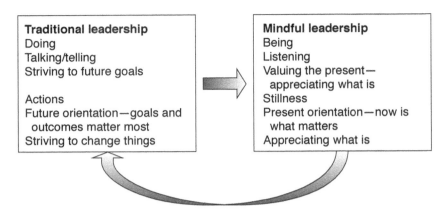

Figure 1: Emphases in traditional versus mindful leadership

With many audiences, I can hear the protests before I invite them: 'But how does anything get done?' 'This is all very well in some environments, but in mine (construction, policing, health or child services, corporate finance, etc.) we've got to deliver things!' They have a point.

However, when we explore further, it is clear that most leaders understand all too well the experience and the problems of spending all one's time in the left-hand column. In too much 'doing', there are feelings of being overwhelmed, of being the only one carrying the load, unable to prioritise or focus or deliver what really matters.

Leadership isn't doing. Even recognising that the pressures of the job or the context have driven people into spending all their energies in the left-hand column is a useful start for many. Finding opportunities, ways of giving themselves permission and space to be in the right-hand column, at least for some of the time, enables leaders to gain perspective and choose which of the 'doing' and 'telling' actually delivers impact.

Throughout this book I suggest that a foundation of leading mindfully is placing value on how one is being—with others and in the moment—as well as doing. What impacts are we having on those around us? What is enabled through us?

Even more powerfully, the possibility is that making the shift to being sometimes allows the doing to 'land' with more impact and resonance. (The arrow returning back from being to doing conveys this in Figure 1.) Being less frenetic, less rushed, enables the doing to be more targeted and more influential. It is also experienced by others as coming from somewhere that is anchored in overarching purpose (see Chapter 16 'Feeling'), rather than just more of the same running. Finding ways of being, and being stiller, in the midst of all the doing, enables actions to be compelling and purposeful. Finding ways to appreciate what is can be a key to enabling people to be open to change.

Two

THINKING LESS

For you to truly be here, thinking has to stop.
Thich Nhat Hanh

Using the mind to think is one of those taken-for-granted activities that we rarely stop to explore or analyse. For most of us schooled in Western notions, there is only consciousness. We have a mind—often equated with the physical brain—which is us. We can't step back from consciousness or observe thinking, it just is.

In contrast, many Eastern philosophies teach that there is the ordinary mind, and another aspect of our mind, which is able with practice to observe and modify the ordinary mind's activities. Increasingly, neuroscientific findings support the latter view and, as I summarise throughout this book, psychologists and others interested in improving how we function, advise us on beneficial ways to direct and modify how we think. Radically, research suggests that leadership might benefit from thinking less, not more, and certainly, thinking differently.

Leading mindfully means using our minds and thinking in both a more discriminating and a more expansive way. Being able to gain perspective on the mind enables leaders to focus their thinking on what matters, less caught up and stressed by the mind's deviations, ruminations and, sometimes, catastrophising. Being able to see beyond the chatter of habitual thinking, we are in turn less of a slave to those thoughts and able to choose if we give them an audience. Becoming more selective in when and how we think also frees our attentional and noticing space—we discover other capacities to access less commonly utilised 'modes' or states of mind, such as reflecting, attending and simple awareness (the subjects of following chapters). Each of these states of mind that are not habitual thinking are additional, valuable and underutilised ways of being in leadership.

A couple of years ago I taught an MBA Leadership and Change subject with a large group that I particularly enjoyed. The participants had demonstrated right from the start an appetite to take risks, be open and share important things about themselves with each other. It doesn't always happen, but with this group it was thrilling and this climate enabled me to be courageous, too.

Towards the end of the ten-class term we began exploring mindfulness and I led the class in a meditation. As part of that I reminded them that 'you are not your thoughts' and you always have the option of observing rather than just being your thoughts. It is a common instruction but, as is sometimes the case, it can land with dazzling impact. 'I am not my thoughts' helped some in this group see what had been stopping them from trying a new career venture. It was the thoughts! The thoughts about 'Who I am', 'What industry I am in', 'What I am good at'. Other habits of thinking that were getting in the way of leadership were, for example, the thoughts that pursuing what one is passionate about, or wanting to work differently, were naïve and unrealistic. For some, my instruction enabled them to see they brought to leadership qualities such as playfulness, creativity and generosity, qualities their usual thoughts had deemed illegitimate in leadership. This moment of mindfulness enabled at least some to see that their habitual thoughts and their usual ways of thinking were not always valuable to them in leadership, and certainly were not the whole of them and their potential value.

WHY LEADERS GET HIJACKED BY THINKING

In my work I come across a lot of clever people who are suffering from their habits of thinking. For many, the capacity to think is what they have been rewarded for—by parents, schools, universities, employers. They bring the same drive to analyse, dissect, problem-solve, to never relinquish thinking, to all aspects of their lives. In very palpable ways, their whole being is fused with their mind. Who am I, they ask, if I'm not my mind, my intellectual firepower?

Growing up I was encouraged, like many young women, to see my brains as the passport to success. I had come from a family of strong women who had never had the opportunity of an education. One great aunt ran a pub, another was a radio announcer and my grandmother was a voracious reader with opinions on everything (perhaps that's where I get it from!). My mother was a super-smart student of Latin and languages, but it took her until well into her 30s to break out from 1950s suburban domesticity and go to university. The neighbours, her friends and my father were mystified. But the women of the family cheered. A vivid early memory was accompanying her to an Old English tutorial, watching the dust mites as sunlight penetrated the leadlights of a worn-out tutorial room, but sensing there was something important happening here. Further education was a good decision on my mum's part. She finished university and qualified as a teacher about a year before my dad died suddenly, leaving us drastically in need of a regular income.

I was also a 'late developer' and a third born, after two brothers: I was often overlooked, literally not seen by family or teachers. You can understand why I became very identified with my brain and my capacity to think as a passport to recognition and success. In my experience working with leaders, and perhaps particularly young women who might not attract mentors or opportunities for leadership, working hard and cultivating one's capacity to think becomes who they are. But at a particular stage in my own life and career, thinking of myself as just good at thinking started to become a problem for me. I only valued my thinking self. While that thinking mind was a marvellous tool, it had taken up complete occupancy, becoming an obstacle to, not a supporter of, my happiness and success in a broader sense.

For myself, and for some leaders with whom I work, exploring and *experiencing* mindfulness is a key to putting the thinking mind into perspective, to experimenting with bringing into leadership other aspects and ways of being. I put the emphasis here on experiencing because some of what mindfulness offers is not accessible by thinking about it! Mindfulness isn't just another form of thinking. As I suggest in the rest of this book, leading mindfully is about being open to allowing other parts of us in to play.

PHILOSOPHY AND RESEARCH ABOUT THE MIND

Many, very different, bodies of knowledge contribute insights to how the mind and thinking work in leadership. Developments in neuroscience and cognitive psychology over the last few decades have grown exponentially, providing vast new knowledge about the operation of the brain and neural systems in activities such as decision-making and responding with emotional intelligence.

Among the most important findings of this work is 'neural plasticity', that is, the brain and the body's neural structures are capable of high levels of adaption over the entire life course.

Thus, all of us (even those unkindly labelled 'past it' by our juniors) have the capacity to see, and to change, the way we think. For example, researchers such as economics Nobel laureate Daniel Kahneman[1] and popular writers such as Malcolm Gladwell distinguish between fast intuitive responses—which Gladwell calls 'blinking'[2]—and more considered, deliberative thinking. Most helpfully for leadership, this research reveals that traditionally privileged ways of thinking—conscious and effortful—are not as rational, or unbiased, or reliable, as we thought! Kahneman's prize-winning work shows that our thinking self, especially if it involves memory and evaluation, systematically distorts actual experience, often in negative and unhelpful ways.

To use an example from my own experience, I was given the opportunity to work with a senior group of medical specialists just after I'd finished teaching a very different group, some of whom rated my capabilities and the value of the subject poorly. In preparing for teaching the medical group, I found myself evaluating the new opportunity based on two remembered moments: how the recent teaching experience ended and its most intense (difficult) moment (the 'peak/end' rule). As Kahneman predicts, the *remembered* experiences drove out the *moment-by-moment* experiences which may be, and in this case were, actually largely effective and enjoyable. According to Kahneman this process—ubiquitous as it is—often leads us to make bad choices. In my case it meant that I was dreading the new opportunity until I paused, noticed where my thoughts and remembering self were taking me, and made a more mindful choice to be open to whatever the new group presented. This helped me be less fearful and the experience unfolded as quite challenging but rewarding and pleasurable too.

In other work with his colleague Jason Riis, Kahneman writes about their research and titles a chapter 'Living and thinking about it: Two perspectives on life'. It powerfully encapsulates that living is not always enriched by thinking. It is important to value experience independently of our thoughts about it. In fact, Kahneman and Riis go on to elaborate that our well-being is determined by two factors: the moment-by-moment feelings and enjoyment; and, only second, our deliberative assessment of our life satisfaction. This research provides powerful reason and evidence to *rethink* our assumptions about the quality and value of thinking. From the perspective of mindfulness though, we need to recognise that this activity may be just better thinking about thinking.[3] The point here is that while thinking better is valuable, thinking less may be more likely to be the route to mindfulness.

Another source of research and knowledge about the mind comes from philosophy, such as Buddhist and yoga philosophy, and areas of consciousness studies. These draw on centuries, perhaps millennia, of practitioner experiments in accessing the mind's workings. While neuroscience is largely (though not exclusively) concerned with the brain and its wiring[4], more ancient philosophies focus on the mind. In these traditions, the mind is different from, and more than, the brain. The mind can observe and discriminate among perceptions, thoughts and sensations.[5] Neural pathways that exist in the heart and rest of our body equip us with intelligence and memory that is accessed in our functioning. A useful way to distinguish the mind and brain comes from Craig Hassed, a medical academic and long-term scholar of mind-body relationships. He defines the brain as the physical organ which translates thought and emotion into electrical, biological and chemical activity and subsequently regulates other body functions. The mind is non-physical, constituted by thought and emotion. Hassed reminds us that 'a major part of what is happening in the brain is based on belief rather than chemicals'[6].

In many Eastern philosophies the mind is not located in the brain—rather, it may be associated with the heart or other regions of the body. Further, while Western understandings generally assume humans have one brain/mind, Eastern understandings are that we are possessed of many minds. For example, Buddhist teachings help us recognise when our 'monkey' mind becomes dominant: proliferating chatter, easily distracted, grasping at thoughts. Yoga philosophy teaches there is *manas* (the managing, traffic-directing mind), *ahamkara* (the mind that is ego-centred and worried about the self), and *buddhi* (the more discriminating and potentially enlightened mind).

As I explore further in the next chapter, most of us can readily begin to recognise different qualities in our thinking and can notice when our mind has been taken over by, for example, the monkey mind. In this moment of recognition, we are reminded that other more spacious mind states are always there waiting for us to come back to. In Buddhism, simple spacious mindfulness *is* the nature of our minds. It is not hard to find. We don't have to work hard to achieve it.

HOW DOES TOO MUCH THINKING GET IN THE WAY OF LEADERSHIP?

Conventional theory sees thinking as a core part of leadership. It is true that for leadership work we need to absorb and sort data, evaluate and analyse, identify different paths and solve problems. Yet the increasing evidence is that we may think too much. The tendency to think 'excessively' is often a problem for leaders.[7] We might think when we don't need to—at 3 a.m., for example. We might think so compulsively that all that results is feeling anxious and unable to cope. Our habitual thinking patterns may stop us from seeing much more important things.

In my work with managers and executives, one of the things that many *think* about is what others *think* of them. This tendency to worry about what others think of us is widespread. Studies show that most of us do it and all of us wish we did less of it. It is true that common advice tells aspiring leaders that they've got to worry about how they come across (this is discussed further in Chapter 17 'Being ourselves?'). The advice goes like this: You've got to cultivate the right kind of behaviour and 'look' to be seen by others as 'a team player', a 'self-starter' or 'results-oriented'. These prescriptions can be highly specific— for women, it can come down to the heel height of their shoes, the amount of jewellery or how often they wear black (and more on this in Chapter 12 'Looking after bodies').

Yet the evidence is that all this thinking and then trying to 'fit' by planning and adapting one's style to the norm is rarely judged or experienced as successful. 'She's trying to be too like one of the boys,' men complain when women join the footy-tipping comp or gatecrash the golf game. To some degree men, too, get penalised when they too eagerly mimic their boss's habits or spend excessive effort second-guessing how they should come across. Research undertaken by one of my doctoral students, Alyson Meister, shows that aspiring leaders can get trapped in experiences of what she calls 'identity asymmetry': that is, in chronic experiences of feeling that others see them in skewed ways, and not as they see themselves.

While there is extensive research on this topic of identity mismatch, Alyson's qualitative research provides a window to how minds and thoughts get recruited to this experience— (mis)interpreting signals, second-guessing, trying to please, and feeding internalised doubts and stress about one's belonging, competence and value—which in turn produces negative impacts

on well-being and performance. Being preoccupied with antici-
pating or fearing what others might think of us produces other
bad outcomes for leadership. It stops people voicing observations and perceptions that depart from the norm. It leads to
groupthink, or a herd mentality.

Even more significantly, Alyson's research identifies that
those who actually perform best are less bothered by assessing
how others see them and the discrepancy between their own and
others' view of self. The findings from this research highlight
the ill-effects from conforming pressures that stop people being
courageous and effective in their roles. More than this, though, it
shows how habitual or excessive thinking exacerbates the experience. Some leaders, over the course of leadership careers, come
to gain perspective on being held hostage not just by the experience but also by their thoughts about it. But for others there is
no gap between 'who I am' (including 'how valuable and competent I am') and 'my thoughts about how others see me'.

Thinking may not be the only way, or even a good way, to
solve difficult challenges in leadership.[8] Researchers in various
areas of decision-making confirm the risks of leaders living too
much in their thoughts. Habitual processes that are rewarded
in organisational contexts such as conceptualisation, commitment and even striving towards authenticity may undermine,
not support, leaders to undertake difficult challenges. How does
this occur?

A significant body of research has been undertaken exploring
organisational or collective mindfulness and its impacts on
decision-making, innovation and crisis management. While
the definition of mindfulness used in this research is closer to
psychologist Ellen Langer's definition described earlier (what
some distinguish as a 'Western' versus 'Eastern' notion[9]), there
are many valuable insights from this work about the pressures
leaders experience to collude with mindlessness and about how

they can foster both 'organisational mindfulness' and 'mindful organising'.[10] For example, according to researchers Karl Weick and Ted Putnam, because organisations are established, held together and made effective largely by means of concepts, leaders and managers tend to jump to premature conclusions about what they are witnessing and they don't register other phenomena. They cling to various definitions of 'the situation' and understandings of their own identity and role in 'the situation' as if they are permanent and fixed. These researchers identify that, perversely perhaps, the more leaders strive for behavioural commitment, the less mindful they can become.

Further, and while there is a place for rational planning and strategising, researchers in the fields of disaster management show that sometimes thinking routines of planning and safety audits actually induce a kind of mindlessness (see Chapter 9 'Being mindful in crises'). What high-risk environments may actually need is a consistently high level of awareness, as if one keeps seeing circumstances with fresh eyes and is therefore able to notice small warning signals, and react quickly to unexpected variations in conditions.

Finely honed habits of thinking that initially provide for leadership success can thus become a liability if they dominate to the exclusion of other ways of being. For example, dreadful things happen to us and around us—serious illness and accidents, family breakdowns, loss of loved ones—according to people who study stress reactions. Yet the duration and depth of experienced stress are likely to be less a product of these events and more a result of our thinking repetitively or ruminatively. In a very real way, suffering and anxiety is determined by thinking patterns, not what happens to us.

STEPPING BACK FROM THINKING
IN LEADERSHIP

So, if thinking is sometimes not useful for leaders, what are the alternatives?

Leadership author David Rock suggests that a key role leaders can play is to help others 'think about thinking'—not just think themselves.[11] In any interaction this might include the following:

- Encourage and support others to do the thinking, don't tell them what to do.
- Focus on their thinking, not the issue on the table, help them make new connections (these may or may not be visible to you), put process before content.
- Remember to stretch.
- 'Accentuate the positive' by being appreciative, validating, affirming, recognising and thanking.

An example of how these insights can 'land' usefully for leaders comes from some of the school principals who attend our leadership programs. Principals run huge operations, sometimes with hundreds of highly qualified specialised staff, thousands of students, opinionated stakeholders, large capital works programs and requirements to raise funds in order to continue to operate. They are in an environment where management and leadership are not necessarily valued. Yet they need to back themselves and encourage their colleagues to step out of the day-to-day pressures to foster collegiality, openness to innovation, and the ability to be moved and inspired by what might be seen as just another cohort of students. Introducing mindfulness often helps them see that they can bring more than their usual, intelligent and adept problem-solving thinking selves to the table and the classroom. They see the patterns in their own way of thinking about problems. This can include seeing with fresh eyes obstacles that are not really obstacles. They are able to be bolder, not so bothered by what others think of them, or what they think others will think of them. They appreciate and express an appreciation of what is around them—the students who surprise and amaze them—and the importance of the enterprise they are embarked on. These shifts depend not on thinking in a new way—such a move would not last—but on being in their world differently. The shifts depend on subtle changes in how awareness and attention is given, how to reflect on self in a way that empowers others, and how to listen more generously.

While thinking is a very central and important activity for leaders, I've offered evidence in this chapter that we over-rely on it. Our thinking is often not so great. But we fall back on it because we believe it's us, or at least it's the value that we bring.

The rest of this book is largely about what else we can bring, what ways of being—other than thinking—might help us be effective, empowering and contented in our leadership. Being mindful in leadership thus encompasses more than thinking. Leading mindfully invites us to experiment with other states of mind and ways of being that bring valuable and refreshing possibilities to contexts that require our attention, our best efforts and our leadership.

Three

LETTING AWARENESS ARRIVE

Your awareness is a very big space within which to reside.
It is never not an ally, a friend, a sanctuary, a refuge.
And it is never not here, only sometimes veiled.
Jon Kabat-Zinn

In my coaching and leadership development work, I often introduce the distinction between thinking, reflecting and awareness. With a small amount of discussion and practice, most individuals can readily notice whether they are in any of these three states of mind at a particular moment (see Figure 2: Different modes of mind).

We discuss and identify the features of thinking: lots of thoughts, moving fast and likely to be repetitive. The same thoughts circulate, coming back for us to think about them again. Part of us might notice ourselves thinking something like, 'If I just think about that once more, I'll definitely get this sorted.' In thinking, we might also notice an orientation towards problem identification and solving. At its most excessive there is also problem creation. For example, we are disturbed in the middle of the night and arrive back into consciousness. Often, within seconds, we have found ourselves a problem where there was none before—an

Awareness	Expansive, open, noticing Not trying to change things
Reflecting	How am I thinking at the moment? Why am I thinking about that in the way I am right now?
Thinking	Evaluative, analytical, problem-solving Fast, may be repetitive, ruminative, catastrophising

Figure 2: Different modes of mind

email, a piece of feedback, a phone call that wasn't made to a parent or family member. In thinking, there is likely to be an analytical, evaluative or judgemental flavour. Indeed, when we are thinking, our thoughts can take on a ruminative or catastrophising quality. Because of these common features, it's generally not hard to be able to notice 'I am thinking now'.

Reflecting is a different state of mind, involving slowing down and putting the 'I' into the mind's equation (also see Chapter 5 'Reflecting on identity with less ego'). When we are reflecting we are asking ourselves questions like: Why am I thinking about that in the way that I am right now? How has the way that person acts come to be a 'hot button' for me? Why is that event 'rattling my cage' and getting such a strong reaction from me at the moment?

Reflecting is a vital activity for all of us. In a sense, it is the underpinning of all deeper learning where an idea we are exposed to gets adapted in the light of our pre-existing understandings and experience, then internalised as our knowing. Like thinking, it is partially an intellectual process but is also likely to involve emotion and the senses.

The purpose of differentiating mind 'states' is not to say one is better than another or to argue that these are the only places for the mind to be. Rather, each state can be noticed, and experimenting with noticing can assist with leadership work. For example, an over-reliance on thinking means that important cues in the situation or people around us may be missed.

We may get caught up and stressed about a situation we can do nothing about. An absence of reflection means old patterns, which may no longer be functional or sustainable for us, we keep repeating.

Another mind state that is not difficult to notice when we are in it is awareness, also known as mindful awareness. In awareness, our mind is likely to feel open and accepting, even appreciative. We might notice the salty smell in the air, the colour of a winter sky, the pageant of humanity in a train carriage. The mind is not jumping to judgement, problem-solving or trying to change things, but allows things to be as they are, including oneself. In awareness, we often notice things that may have always been there, but we were too caught up in our thinking to notice before. As explored in Parts Two and Three of this book, reliable ways to come into awareness are via the senses—stopping to see, listen, smell, touch, taste or feel something on our bodies—or via the breath, just noticing the in breath, then the out breath.

Many meditation traditions encourage a practice of watching, and not intervening with thought, through cultivating awareness. It has been described as like standing by a busy road and watching various thoughts rush past like traffic, but not jumping in trying to stop them or divert them to a different path. A more classic analogy described in Sogyal Rinpoche's *The Tibetan Book of Living and Dying* is that awareness is like being located in a vast blue sky, like being in a plane which passes up above the clouds, allowing us to observe thoughts passing, like clouds, without getting involved in them. Also like clouds, thoughts may temporarily obscure but this does not change the awareness that is always there, above or behind them.

Sometimes when I sit to meditate, my mind ramps up, dancing around, doing somersaults and triple backflips to provide incontrovertible proof of how necessary and/or beguilingly clever it is: 'Look at me! I'm important! I've got things to remind you about. Don't ignore me . . . You might get it wrong if you don't pay attention to me, craft that email carefully, go over those events last week one more time . . . And hang on . . . That was an amazing thought! You'll forget it if you don't keep thinking about it for a bit longer . . . Just think about me for a minute, then you can keep meditating . . .'

And so on, and so on. Sometimes I get hooked, and I start going with that attention-hungry mind. But usually I can begin to just notice these desperate efforts to impress me with their ever more world-stopping or supposedly remarkable character. As I do so they usually slow down, and lose their anxiety-provoking or grabbing quality. At other times, it helps for me to be the observer and have a quiet conversation with the mind: 'You can relax now. You can go offline. You've done enough thinking about that. Just rest.' With this encouragement, I often feel my whole body, including inside my head, soften and melt. A whole body warmth and softness envelopes . . . for a few moments at least.

Neuroscientific research documents how our brain responds in these processes of quieting or barely observing the thinking mind. Key parts of the frontal cortex responsible for reasoning, planning and conscious thought show marked decrease in activation. There is less beta brain wave activity and more theta activity, eliciting decreases in mental 'noise', increased relaxation, emotional regulation and self-awareness. In therapeutic contexts, this kind of mindfulness is sometimes described using the visual metaphor of noticing how habitual thinking patterns are like grooves or well-worn paths through our neural circuitry. Familiar routes, such as blaming ourselves or taking up a victim space, are easy to go down. However, with mindfulness comes the possibility of seeing the path and not going down it again. With awareness and time, new grooves can be created which are less judgemental and more self-affirming.

Four

GIVING ATTENTION

Attention is the currency of leadership.
Ron Heifetz

Attention—where and how it is given to what—is a key part of what leaders can bring to a situation. Indeed some leadership researchers argue that a leader's foremost 'currency' is not the usual mechanisms such as capabilities in strategy formulation or decision-making, but attention.[1] This includes deploying the leader's own attention wisely and shaping where others in their organisations and environments give, and focus, their attention.

Giving attention might be as simple as focusing your full attention on someone who comes to see you with a problem. It might mean not checking your phone in a meeting or during a conference call. But I would also like to suggest something further in this chapter. Our very notions or experiences of attention are themselves stunted or have been corrupted. We've forgotten or never really been helped to learn how to give whole-hearted attention. As children, we may never have experienced it from family members or teachers.

An example of this comes from the research of an Australian doctoral student. For several years I have enjoyed exploring leadership with Indigenous doctoral students as part of a Graduate Certificate in Indigenous Research & Leadership at Melbourne University. The groups I teach comprise students working across faculties and areas and, on one particular occasion, when we were discussing attention and listening, one of the women volunteered her own research with Aboriginal children. Her finding was that children rarely had the benefit of being listened to or given full attention. Typically, the source of this kind of attention only came from grandparents and if children didn't get it, they never developed the confidence to feel they would be heard. As I discuss further in Chapter 6 'Listening from stillness', Australian Indigenous cultures, and especially their elders, often offer a version of mindful listening known as *dadirri*. According to this researcher's findings, experiencing good quality, patient attention from older relatives was pivotal to children's well-being and their psychological and educational futures.

One of the first Australian organisations dedicated to introducing mindfulness in workplaces is Mind Gardener, which is based in Queensland. According to founders Susan Pearse and Martina Sheehan, the act of paying attention is an act of care.[2] It signifies that you regard someone as important or interesting. And attention is the medium of exchange of everything worthwhile in life: learning, love, guidance, beauty, awe.

You may have noticed that I have used the term 'giving attention' rather than the more common phrase 'paying attention'. As I wrote this book and explored the meanings of mindfulness in leadership, I felt that 'paying' was the wrong verb. Paying attention is important in mindfulness but giving attention is an underrated part of leadership.

HOW MIGHT GIVING ATTENTION HELP
LEADERS?

Research consistently shows that most of us deliver a very poor quality of attention and we find it hard to focus our attention on what we are doing. Researcher of attention B. Alan Wallace maintains that most people struggle to hold their attention on one thing for more than about 3–5 seconds. For example, in a typical meeting, our minds might be thinking about lunch, the weekend that just sped by and whether that remark ten minutes ago by the CEO should be taken personally, despite our efforts to focus on an issue being discussed.

Difficulties with paying attention has consequences for emotional health and effectiveness. In their research on the costs of multitasking, McKinsey researchers Derek Dean and Caroline Webb find that such habits of hovering poor quality attention on multiple issues reduces efficiency, not enhances it.[3] They also note that while the capacity to multitask is often a badge of achievement in workplaces, it reduces job satisfaction and experienced feelings of health and well-being. Constantly moving one's attention between tasks and people, for most of us, increases feelings of stress and anxiety (despite or perhaps because it is addictive), and it results in lower productivity. A study of 2250 volunteers who were prompted throughout the day by their phone found that almost half the time people's minds were not on what they were doing.[4] Further, at this time when their minds and their bodies were in different places, only 56 per cent reported feeling happy, compared to 66 per cent of those whose minds were on what they were doing.

Other managerial decision-making research shows just how readily attention gets diverted not by external factors but by our own thinking. In their research on cognitive decision-making, scholars C. Marlena Fiol and Edward O'Connor note that information-rich environments characterise the world of executives today. What determines their effectiveness is not access to information but the amount of focused attention that decision-makers allocate to making that information meaningful. The human mind *and* body are key factors determining which features of any decision context gain attention. Thus decision-makers 'mentally and socially construct the realities that later constrain them'.[5]

Practising mindfulness through, for example, regular meditation, significantly improves our capacity to focus and sustain attention. Mindfulness trains people to increase their capacity to pay attention—beyond the 3–5 seconds that is normal—and also to develop different *qualities* of attention for different situations. For example, and building on Buddhist teachings, Wallace has differentiated:

- qualities of attentional ease (an open relaxed noticing)
- attentional stability (being able to sustain focused attention on one object)
- attentional vividness (being awake and energised to all that's there).

Wallace also draws on studies of creativity, showing that people who we consider geniuses across many fields often share a capacity to maintain attention and clarity over long periods. He calls this capability 'alert equipoise'.

The capacity to give different qualities of attention to different aspects of context is highly relevant for leaders who often face multiple competing demands on their attention. A common response to attentional demands that I see in my work with leaders is hypervigilance—constant surveillance and a high-alert default mindset. Hypervigilance can seep into leadership teams and staff, so that threats and risks are seen to be coming from everywhere. No-one can switch off. Paradoxically, though, this high arousal state where everything is worried about does not necessarily deliver good crisis prevention or management (as explored in Chapter 9 'Being mindful in crises'). Rather, attention is so tight and unrelaxed that it misses small but important pieces of data or feedback.

An example of how giving attention can support leadership to be innovative is described by Jon Kabat-Zinn in his book *Coming to Our Senses*. Zindel Segal, Mark Williams and John Teasdale, an internationally renowned group of researchers of mechanisms to relieve clinical depression, approached Kabat-Zinn because they were interested in developing a mindfulness-based cognitive therapy. However, as Kabat-Zinn notes, their own habits of thinking and allocating attention were initially major obstacles. It was only after lots of talking, suspending their own professional frameworks in studying and helping people cope with depression, including their own view of themselves and how researchers should act; and, importantly, committing to trying mindfulness for themselves, that this group were able to pioneer a completely new approach to depression. Part of the move they had to make was to themselves shift from a *doing* and *fixing* orientation, to a *being* one, and a being one that is interested in 'non-doing'. Importantly, the way they made this shift was to pay attention to their own processes of awareness, to experiment through meditation with 'bare, non-judgemental, non-reactive, non-conceptual attention'.[6] In Kabat-Zinn's terms, they could not get 'there' (the therapeutic tool they were seeking) from 'here' (where they were standing and with their habitual modes of thinking).

Sometimes, perhaps even often, leadership requires us to 'think outside of the box'. As writers such as Steven Pinker show, it is very difficult for many of us to *see* our thinking, and to appreciate the extent to which habitual thinking limits what we can see and know. The above example illustrates how leadership innovation requires us to shed our usual lenses, to even 'dial down' the identity of the looker wearing the lens (the subject of Chapter 5 'Reflecting on identity with less ego'). The way these researchers did this was not to keep researching and testing but to pay attention to 'the unfolding of their own direct experience from moment to moment'.[7]

In their crisis-management research identifying the characteristics of High Reliability Organisations (or HROs), Karl Weick and his colleagues suggest that, to reduce the likelihood of disasters, individuals need to be trained to pay attention and organisations need to develop 'collective mindfulness' (see Chapter 9 'Being mindful in crises' for more on this). The work of Harvard health professor, surgeon and author Atul Gawande provides another powerful example.[8] Gawande began his research with the observation that around the world, the success rate of surgery is poor and it does not necessarily correlate with the amount of money being spent, the level of training or the technology available to surgical teams. He believes that poor and not improving surgical performance is rooted in dramatically increasing complexity that surgeons and their teams now face.

What does he advocate in response? This is the interesting part and where paying attention and mindfulness play key roles. With the help of leaders across many different fields of endeavour, Gawande developed simple checklists that he recommends all surgical teams follow. These checklists include items that doctors and nurses already know about; for example, how quickly a post-surgery patient gets their antibiotic. However, it is the *process* of administering the checklist publicly that is where mindfulness comes in.

First, everyone in the room is identified and their role clarified. Gawande found that due to medical hierarchies and habit this wasn't always the case—people didn't always know the names or roles of others in the room. Who was responsible for critical monitoring was sometimes not clear. Second, there are identified *pause points*: points of stopping and paying very focused attention. These are moments when any individual is encouraged to recognise a risk and do something about it. Because the pause points are built into the protocols, any individual can raise a concern without it being a criticism of someone else in the room. A third feature of these protocols, that is also one of the big obstacles to their implementation, is that their very simplicity requires those involved in complex operations to drop their individual expert mindset and, in the moment, recognise that they are all interdependent in creating a good outcome. Values of humility, teamwork and an openness to seeing what one might not otherwise are therefore built into the process. Gawande provides an example from his own practice where, by inviting a colleague to watch him operate, he became aware of a number of things he did that he could improve on. For example, he held his elbow and arm in an awkward way, and his focus of attention on the patient's progress needed to be wider at particular stages of the surgery.

Despite the protocols dramatically reducing death rates and serious mishaps from surgery in many locations around the world, Gawande notes that the final shift—of mindset and values towards mindfulness in the moment-by-moment of surgery—is the hardest to make and the source of most resistance among doctors and other medical professionals. Here, he is also interested in a key plank of Buddhist conceptions of mindfulness: the readiness to explore death and mortality, and the belief that doing so helps us come to grips with our own humanity, fallibility and ignorance. Being open to considering mortality is a very valuable thing for leaders. For Gawande, it helps medical and health professionals focus on their moral goals and what, in the final analysis, they are wanting to contribute to and help change. It helps them get in touch with their own fallibility, making them more human and braver in having conversations with patients.

HOW TO GIVE ATTENTION

As discussed above, the main obstacles in giving attention are in our own mind. They are the other thoughts that bulldoze or beguile their way in, diverting our attention to them: 'I haven't got time for this now', 'I can't sit around all day listening to this'.

It takes conscious practice to get better at holding attention on one object for a sustained time. It is this activity of keeping attention focused on one object, such as the breath, sounds, the body, or an image of a guru or teacher, that is the foundation step of most meditation traditions. Research studies which monitor the results of meditation in novice practitioners find that an improved capacity to focus attention is one of the most reliable, consistently experienced outcomes.

Further, the work of B. Alan Wallace shows that, with practice, different dimensions of attention, such as attentional stability, vividness or clarity, also begin to develop.

In Buddhist meditation traditions, the culmination of practice in directing and focusing attention is *shamatha*, also known as 'calm abiding'. In his book *The Attention Revolution*, Wallace draws on the work of the eighth-century Indian contemplative scholar Kamalashila, in his *Stages of Meditation*, to identify many subtle qualities of attention:

1. Directed attention
2. Continuous attention
3. Resurgent attention
4. Close attention

5. Tamed attention
6. Pacified attention
7. Fully pacified attention
8. Single-pointed attention
9. Attentional balance
10. *Shamatha.*

As I noted earlier, and despite being a meditator for ten years, I regard myself as a novice in attentional stability and balance. Yet when I was introduced to and had glimpses of experiencing 'calm abiding' or *shamatha*—for example, under the guidance of Buddhist teacher Sogyal Rinpoche[9]—I have found it to be a profound touchstone in my meditation and in my life. In calm abiding, we are not striving or clinging to things, not trying to get to some better state or place, even a more advanced state of meditation! Rather, the mind is experienced as clear and present, undisturbed by the mind's shenanigans. When meditating in the Buddhist tradition, we are encouraged to have 25 per cent of our attention lightly on technique, and 25 per cent attention on mindfulness of that technique, such as noticing when our attention strays from the breath. The remaining 50 per cent is in simple spaciousness.

One metaphor that is used across different meditative traditions visualises the mind as a pool of water which, if left without stirring or prodding (thinking about it), becomes clear. For me personally, allowing myself time to simply sit in a state I associate with 'calm abiding' feels nourishing and clarity inducing. Just letting myself be, letting my mind soften and release its grip, letting my body be in whatever state it is, I don't need to think about anything or do anything.

Leadership researchers also document the value for leaders of cultivating the capacity to give quality attention. For example, leadership academic Judi Marshall has written extensively about action-learning, or developing habits of learning in the midst of doing. She describes this as a way of life or as 'living life as inquiry'. Elements include:

- opening what one knows, feels, does and wants to question and inquiry
- proceeding with respectful intent and purpose
- treating little (of what one sees or knows) as fixed
- valuing the integrity of what is present before you with its unfolding process
- honing 'inner arcs of attention': attending to one's own assumptions, patterns, sense-making habits asking 'what is my stuff?' or 'what parts of this experience am I bringing and not owning?'
- developing 'outer arcs of attention': inquiring with others, turning issues and puzzles into collaborative, engaged inquiries
- treating what emerges as important data: being non-judgemental, knowing when to persist and when to desist.[10]

Marshall thus encourages leaders to notice what is happening internally and bodily, asking questions such as 'How am I responding to this now?' or 'How am I hearing what is being said and what might be shaping that?' Building on Marshall's work, ethical leadership scholar Donna Ladkin argues that cultivating finer attention to inner and outer conditions is an important basis for moral judgement and action. In a quite radical reorientation from traditional approaches of teaching managerial ethics through philosophical theories, Ladkin argues a foundational step is simply improving the quality of noticing and attention.

For all of us, there are valuable insights and reasons to experiment with giving better attention, drawing from the diverse traditions of research described in this chapter. We don't need to go anywhere special, or wait for particular conditions, to practise this. We don't need to meditate to give attention. It's actually a very simple practice or decision which you might like to experiment with over the course of the next few hours:

Step 1: Invite yourself to hold attention on something or, even better, someone who is saying something potentially important.

Step 2: Notice if or when thoughts, evaluations or premature conclusions arise as you are attending. Just let them be there lightly.

Step 3: Use external sounds or your breath or your body to bring you back into the present moment of giving attention. Allow your senses, rather than your thoughts, to help you remain attentive.

Five

REFLECTING ON IDENTITY
WITH LESS EGO

We walk through so many myths of each other
and ourselves.
Natalie Goldberg

Why might leaders benefit from reflecting on identity? Isn't that just 'navel-gazing',[1] and more appropriate for therapy than leadership? In this chapter I suggest that reflecting on who and how we are being in leadership—our identity—is a core part of helping free ourselves to be engaged and fulfilled in leadership, while also being helpful and present for others.

Reflection is different to many other leadership capabilities, such as listening, observing and talking. As the basis of all deep learning, reflecting involves an extra 'loop'[2] where we assess what we hear or read in the context of what we already know. As we translate new ideas and concepts into our 'language' and systems of meaning, we make them our own. In this way, theoretical ideas or knowledge becomes personally generated insight with the potential to be transformative and empowering.

Reflecting can take many forms but the one I focus on in this chapter is reflection about self. This includes the sources and pressures of our multiple and dynamic identities from our background and history—what is sometimes called identity work in the leadership literature. It includes reflection-in-action, seen by some theorists as equivalent to mindfulness. Reflection-in-action occurs in the moment, for example, as we notice that we are repeating a pattern of reaction that derives from history.[3] Further, though, mindfulness offers the opportunity to observe and make good choices about ego needs, rather than being unconsciously trapped by, or in, them.

Introducing and working with leaders on reflection and identity has become a key part of what I do with MBA and executive groups, as well as in coaching individuals. In this chapter, I share some examples of the diverse ways this work unfolds and the effects on participants. The process is emergent, depending on what has gone before, how long we have together as a group, and the interests and openness of the individuals and group-as-a-whole, which generally become quickly apparent. However, in each case there are elements such as:

- Encouraging participants to shift their attention from what they are doing in leadership to how they are being, suggesting (as I do in earlier chapters of this book) that sometimes ways of being are central to influence and effectiveness.
- Introducing ideas about identity and identity work, such as that we typically inhabit multiple identities and experience cultural, social, professional and organisational pressures to perform particular leadership identities. Leadership is then understood as not just a role or position, but brings with it an assemblage of internal and external pressures on identity, including particular templates of what good leadership will look like in different contexts.

- Exercises designed to help participants reflect on the sources of their own leadership identities. Noticing the narratives or scripts that they have been given or internalised for how they should *be* and how they should be as leaders. These exercises are usually done in pairs and involve deep and sometimes emotional explorations of families, schooling, professional training, crises or 'crucibles'[4] in their lives and careers. Such past experiences have often left a template for how leaders feel they *should be*, which has typically been treated as reality that is not available for modification.

- Sharing examples of crisis and failure from my own career (and there are many from which to choose!) where I have become caught up in a loop of recrimination and self-blame, invested in defending and protecting myself. The moment of insight occurs when I recognise that I don't have to put all my energies into securing myself in the face of this difficult experience; that this process of rumination that I am generating is just thoughts. I have a choice about whether to stay trapped in these recursive thoughts or to step into a bigger space of being. Once I share examples of this kind of experience, a discussion often unfolds where people recognise their own instances of being caught in that loop of ego. We talk about how to make the move out of it, including discussions of learning, letting go, finding compassion for self and, most powerfully, the insight from mindfulness that perhaps there is no solid immutable self that needs securing.

How does this material about reflection, identity and ego 'land' with leadership groups? The Williamson Community and Folio Leadership Programs in Melbourne provide corporate, public sector and community leaders with an opportunity to work together and develop their appetite and skills for community leadership. Generally, when I join them to facilitate a half-day session, they have already worked a lot together and been exposed to some dynamic community leaders. I facilitate a session entitled 'Going Back to Go Forward' (also a chapter of my book *Leadership for the Disillusioned*).

The discussion and exercises often enable leaders to identify patterns from the past, such as ways of thinking about themselves, which they continue to re-enact, yet may be getting in the way of their leadership. An example is assuming the 'responsible-for-everyone' oldest child role, or it might be continuing to achieve or mould oneself to a corporate or bureaucratic norm to gain approval or win belonging. Reflecting can help individuals notice how readily they move into their familiar positions. They might both see the pattern and see that the pattern has become part of identity: 'That's who I am/That's what I do'. The process can enable a third, most freeing, step which is to recognise that 'This is just a bundle of thoughts', 'It's not reality' or 'It's not me', 'I don't need to repeat this, I am more than this pattern', or 'I can add new and different value here'.

As sessions unfold, ideas and practices from mindfulness support the process. While the primary purpose is to invite people to reflect on their identity and how it has been shaped, mindfulness often enables them to disentangle themselves from their thinking about 'me'. Being encouraged to identify and label the pressures on us to produce a certain identity or self in leadership creates a different space which one can inhabit in leadership and groups. Being less involved in this production of our own needs and views makes us more available for others and the issues of the present moment.

Different dynamics and insights arise in work with other groups. The Victorian and Tasmanian branches of the Australian

Education Union has invited me to be part of their WILD (Women in Leadership Development) program for several years. WILD has been designed to encourage highly capable women teachers to take on principal and deputy principal roles in primary and secondary state schools and the early childhood education system. I have worked with several cohorts of these women in Victoria and Tasmania, generally towards the end of the program, and I have been profoundly moved on many occasions by their commitment to education and their own openness to learning about how to lead change. In one recent group, I asked the women to introduce themselves to me and reintroduce themselves to each other by telling us something about their leadership that others in the room might not already know about them but that is important to understanding their leadership. Many did so by describing their upbringing and parents: mothers who have been pillars of the local community, involved, opinionated and active within the confines of the norms of the 1960s, 1970s and 1980s when these women were growing up. Some fathers were also important in supporting daughters to 'do anything they set their mind to'.

There were high expectations to 'give back' to community in their stories and, to some extent also, stories of how their commitment had been thwarted once they entered teaching, by conservative schools and school leadership structures which didn't recognise their community-mindedness as leadership. Memorably, after numerous examples of hard-working community-minded families, one woman candidly described her dysfunctional family and overbearing father. Upstanding and respectable from the outside, a very different story occurred within domestic walls. She described the legacy for her own approach to leadership: a risk-taking and preparedness to back her intuition that she learned as a survival mechanism in childhood. She both described her approach to leadership and enacted it in that moment of the program by interrupting the dominant group narrative, reminding us of the confronting reality of many people's childhoods. She helped us all get more honest and real. Making a decision to share her experiences with us provided a model of leadership for the group, the grit and intensity of which we experienced very directly.

The identity challenges facing this group of teachers are also common in my coaching work. Leaders, and especially those who are making transitions into larger or more prominent and exposed leadership roles, often feel intense pressure to *be* a certain way in leadership. Leadership is frequently not a label that they have associated with themselves or one that sits comfortably. They look up or around them and see models of leadership that they don't admire or seek to emulate. They often get feedback from others in the workplace that they are 'too emotional' or that they need to 'toughen up'.

The way I can assist most is usually not in helping them problem-solve but in creating a space for reflection and mindfulness about their own approach to leadership. Anna, a senior university academic, came to leadership seeing herself as a strong researcher. The stumbling block for her was imagining how she could do leadership, how she could *be* a leader. For her, leadership was being like her boss, or various other heads of departments or deans. Anna assumed that she had to be like them to lead. Our earliest work together involved some reflection about her own history and where some habits and ways of thinking about herself and her strengths had come from. This provided a platform to help her authorise herself to do leadership in her way, and to trust her very good instincts and skills.

A second, more powerful, insight followed from this. As Anna went about her leadership, people working with and for her would react in ways that were difficult. They would push back, argue or ignore her and keep doing what they had always done. Historically, her tendency would be to internalise these responses and judge herself harshly. However, the insight she had gained from mindfulness was the new possibility of stating clearly and respectfully her point of view but then letting go of any following thoughts and ruminations. Giving herself the option of not taking things personally and moving on felt like a weight had been lifted for her. Her leadership work took less of a toll on her; and others, including her boss, experienced her as direct, positive and effective to be around. Anna has got better and better at these reflections-in-action, noticing how some interactions elicit patterns in her but seeing that she has a choice in how she positions herself and responds.

A critical feature of reflection is that it's not just a cognitive process. This kind of identity work sometimes doesn't turn up anything new. But it does sometimes help leaders to get in touch with the emotion surrounding a response. Because of its focus on being present to whatever comes up, mindfulness encourages leaders to stay with feelings, to not dismiss them or tell themselves they must 'get over it' or 'move on'. It allows feelings of compassion and understanding, which may apply to themselves, as well as others.

On occasion, participants sense an immediate freedom, a 'light bulb' moment, from identity work. It enables them to see that leadership does not mean they are condemned to being trapped in roles or identities that they have come to confuse as them. For one participant who held a senior role in a multinational oil company, the culmination of the work she did over a week-long program was a decision to make a big change, leave her employer and start a consulting business of her own. I remember quite clearly the moments in class and afterwards in discussion with me. She saw a new option, a way of working and being in her life that might bring more happiness and satisfaction. A couple of years later she joined us for our Mindful Leadership program, and she continues to check in, registering the significance of these experiences to her enjoyment now of her life, family and work.

WHAT ABOUT EGO?

So, is this reflective identity work described above just an invitation to self-absorption or narcissism? On the contrary, my experience is that mindfully reflecting on identity provides a way of avoiding being excessively driven by ego, self-absorption or self-enhancement.

Ego is originally a psychoanalytic concept that is now widely used to refer to that conscious part of self-identity concerned with mediating individual needs and desires in the real world. Ego is one's idea and opinion about oneself, including a sense of ability and importance. It is also understood to include the 'needy' part of our identity that asserts what we need or feels hurt or unappreciated at criticism.[5] Over the twentieth century, new views of the individual and their needs came to dominate through various disciplines such as psychology and psychiatry. Commonly, these disciplines developed forms of helping people which strengthened ego, making the self more coherent or resilient. Such work is demonstrably helpful for many people, especially, for example, those who have had traumatic experiences in childhood or those coping with severe stress.

Yet the intent and approach in working with leaders needs to be different. Identity and ego are not the same thing. In Eastern traditions, ego is only a subset of the awareness and consciousness that is available to bring to situations. The reason to engage in reflective practices is not to perform more convincingly a desired or authentic self but to see that one can often be more useful in leadership by putting *less* energy into defending our views and ourselves. Advocating that leaders be mindfully reflective, the intent is to help them free themselves from being too captured by ego.

These views about the self, identity and ego are different from those assumed in most mainstream leadership advice. For example, authentic leadership theory (which I examine again in Chapter 17 'Being ourselves?') argues that effective leaders aim to be consistently and authentically themselves.[6] Although in almost all situations authenticity in a leader is welcome, I have found it is often of more help to leaders to enable them to step back and *see* that some of that identity 'stuff' is unnecessary, just ego at work. This can quite easily be let go, and doing so often enables the leader to be available and to bring new qualities to interactions with others.

Buddhist teachings see the self as a fabrication. Just hold that idea for a moment. It is easy to dismiss it—surely the self is important, solid and real. On the other hand, we can get too involved in 'the story' of ourselves. This almost always causes grief because it encourages us to be prescriptive and judgemental about what we need and the conditions we put on our own happiness. Pausing and recognising, first, how much of our sense of self is produced from an endless stream of thoughts and narratives about who we are and what we need, and second, that it might be helpful to let go of some of that thinking, can be an enormously freeing step. It helps us to see how that part of us invested in self-elaboration, what some label the ego, is neither the whole nor a 'truth' about us: 'Perhaps I need not be, or am not only, that set of stories I tell myself about me.'

By stepping back from these processes of performing and projecting a self, mindfulness gives us ways to notice when a lot of our energy is going into, for example, holding onto or protecting an aspect of self, which, from another point of view, turns out to be a fiction. I'm not suggesting here that opinions and ideas should not be strongly held and passionately advocated as part of leadership. My point is that sometimes we can do leadership and advocacy a whole lot better if there is less ego involved.

Social change activist and author Adam Kahane recommends that leadership often requires us to not plan everything but rather 'unclench, pay attention and take our next best step'. (See also Chapter 12 for a discussion of the usefulness of paying attention to the body in these processes.) Advising 'a lot of intent without a lot of content', Kahane suggests that noticing and releasing attachment helps us be less fearful and anxious.[7]

An example comes from one of my MBA students, an enormously energetic marketing professional who took on a new job in a global pharmaceutical company. She interpreted her new leadership role as requiring her to throw her full 80-hour week commitment behind 'selling' an idea to a part of the business she was leading. While some of her superiors were impressed, she was less successful with her teams until she shifted how she was being to more openness to what they had to bring. Offering a new idea or perspective to a group without too much attachment, but in a spirit of interest and curiosity, is almost always welcomed. It is an antidote to the polarisation and fighting over turf that can sometimes paralyse executive teams.

Right now you might be thinking something like, 'But in my organisation you have to be seen to be really committed to be heard and taken seriously.' The norms of many organisational cultures are that ego drives who is seen and succeeds. At the same time, most of us recognise a lot of suffering occurs when people's selves get fused with solutions, feeling it's their role in life to fight and win battles, and that they have no choice. No-one's interests are served when careers or roles are cut short because individual contribution is equated with a particular solution or workplace regime. Rather, bringing mindfulness to reflection enables us to know ourselves in order to free ourselves from being too ego-driven. Perhaps most importantly in leadership, this supports us to be genuinely there for others.

Six

LISTENING FROM STILLNESS

Listening is far more powerful than talking.
Deep, generous listening is what allows for effective
talking, relating and acting.
Richard Searle

The activity of listening is central to most leadership jobs and most individuals in authority positions do a lot of it. Some indeed say they suffer from listening overload, that staff or colleagues simply download on them—at length! Some leaders admit to us that they have to consciously resist the urge to abbreviate listening. What they really want to do is get to the 'gist' of the issue and give some practical advice. Many dread the topic of listening as they suspect that good listening inevitably takes a lot of time, which they feel they never have enough of.

Despite these misgivings, helping people listen differently and more mindfully often has significant impact on the quality of their relationships and what they can accomplish, in work and outside it. Here, I introduce mindful listening as an under-rated but powerful leadership practice. Mindful listening, or listening from stillness, is an approach that my colleague Richard Searle has developed with myself and others as part of the leadership programs he runs.[1] We have subsequently introduced these forms of listening to many different groups and in this chapter I share some experiences from doing so. I also lay to rest some myths, such as that effective listening requires lots of time and a preparedness to 'feel' exactly what the speaker is feeling.

ACTIVE AND MINDFUL LISTENING

Many leaders we come across have been trained in active listening. Active listening principles include asking open rather than closed questions, and maintaining and projecting engagement with the speaker through an alert bodily posture, perhaps eye contact and verbal prompts. These features are designed to engender in the speaker comfort and the confidence to proceed, if not come up with some solutions to the challenges they are sharing.

But listening mindfully is different to listening actively, and people benefit from understanding both approaches and the differences between them. There are several pitfalls in active listening. The first is that some leaders get so practised at the technique that it becomes a performance. One mindful CEO described this as 'putting my nodding face on'. He went on to observe that under these circumstances the ego takes over, delivering a polished but shallow performance. Wryly, he observed that the coach he was working with wasn't fooled. And this is an important insight— others generally know when we have our 'nodding face' on and know that listening is compromised accordingly.

I want to use the example of my MBA classes to illustrate the distinctions between active and mindful listening, with the benefits that this different kind of listening from stillness can offer. As part of their assessment, the students are asked to identify, and then interview, a leader. I encourage them to choose someone who may not self-identify as a leader, to look beyond corporate and sporting settings for their interviewee, but to choose someone from whose leadership they are interested to learn.

Training the students to conduct these interviews is an important part of preparation, including training in listening, and consciously moderating the amount of speaking and silence they habitually adopt. Many of the students have been trained in listening and already think of themselves as good listeners. Some are quite attached to their listening techniques and to their identities as effective listeners. Part of my preparation with them is, then, interrupting this view or getting them to stop and not just practise what they usually do. Thich Nhat Hanh says that stopping is a vital step in mindfulness.[2] To listen deeply, one needs to be fully present to this unique moment. This requires stopping, consciously making an effort to be in the moment, which he describes as 'deep looking', and not delivering one's usual routine of listening.

Another pitfall can occur for many students where they feel they need to impress their interviewee with their own mastery of the subject matter (of leadership) and speaking too much. Once students have identified a leader and scheduled their interview, some feel that their interviewee is doing them a big favour. This can make them nervous and unctuous—which is not a bad thing, but some spend much of their interview not listening but working to project an image as knowledgeable and capable (perhaps even worthy of hiring!). Thus, in some situations where listening is required, the ego's own needs take over, resulting in not much hearing.

Further, sometimes active listening is used by the listener to reassure themselves that they are attending, rather than to support the speaker. When I introduce mindful listening to executive audiences, some protest, 'Oh but I need to add in the "uh-huhs" and the "yes I know" to reassure the speaker that I am here for them.' These habits are particularly common among women leaders, and research of gender and communication patterns tell us that a lot of active 'fillers' and 'prompts' are part of how women have often been socialised to build intimacy and trust.

In a series of exercises I use with executive groups, one practice involves being silent but being present with their whole body. I ask them to remain silent (so no prompts or supportive noises) and also to consciously 'dial down' their usual body language, too, such as nodding. Participants are invited to evidence their listening through their stillness, rather than verbal reassurance. When we experiment with more mindful listening in this way, it emerges that far from being reassuring, speakers are often distracted by those very prompts that are designed to be encouraging. The verbal additions volunteered by listeners are sometimes experienced by speakers as just the listener's 'stuff'. When listeners don't fill up the conversation with their own prompts or are more sparing, speakers feel encouraged to continue, perhaps pursuing more sensitive or hidden aspects to the issues being discussed.

So, part of helping students and executives listen more mindfully is asking them to tune into and notice in the moment their own urges and needs to be seen as supportive and listening (see Figure 3: Levels of listening). We encourage them to notice when, or if, their own minds become engaged while listening, finding points they recognise or agree with, evaluating or judging what they are hearing. With quite a small amount of practice, most people can tune into these processes in the moment, noticing if there is a ramping up of their own commentary, then letting it go and just listening. There is a sense, then, of listening from a stiller and more powerful place.

A second aspect of helping people listen mindfully is encouraging them to experiment with allowing silence. Like the gender

1. Empathic listening, or hearing not just the words but emotions behind them (feelings have more energy and motivation in them than thoughts).

2. Allow another to finish what they want to say; be giving enough attention to know what they said.

3. Generative listening: not what we listen *to* but what we are listening *for*, instead of listening only for the things we like or agree with, listening for the 'nugget of gold'—the telling insight or experience that has often been buried under words or rationales.

4. Mindful listening: listening *from* stillness, silence and spaciousness; turning down our own reactivity and being open in the moment.

Figure 3: Levels of listening
(Adapted from Searle 2011)

patterns described above, pauses and silence can have cultural roots and meanings. There is sometimes 'push back' from those who, again, have strong attachment to habits of responding, with or without pauses or silence. While these cultural and other conventions need to be respected, work with leaders suggests that there is always room to experiment sensitively with silence. Silence can convey great care and respect for the other, especially if difficult issues or feelings are being discussed. Indeed, most people can nominate someone who really listens to them. Frequently, that listening is characterised by silences and not 'jumping in' or 'jumping to solution' by the listener.

A final part of helping people listen mindfully is to encourage them to listen with their whole body, not just their ears. Listeners can demonstrate that they are there for the speaker with their body, their presence, the gentleness of their gaze, the grace or groundedness with which they are felt to 'be there'. This is not an emotional mirroring or identification with the speaker, rather that speakers simply feel held by the stillness and availability of the listener.

What happens for speakers when they are able to tell a story to someone who is listening mindfully? Even in groups where people are working with effective strangers—the person who happens to be sitting next to them—a strong sense of connection and understanding can be established very quickly. People sometimes come to a leadership program with an issue that for them has a very complex history of players and events. It can feel like it needs an hour to explain! Yet with only a few minutes of high quality, mindful listening, someone who they have never met can understand the issue quickly, get to the heart of what is happening, and after an exercise that might only take five minutes, offer feedback and responses that are useful.

Even more profound is where the quality of the listening enables the speaker to find a new insight or way forward on the issue. One EMBA student volunteered that having a listener who was experienced by him as still and unjudging helped him to notice, and then let go of, his usual habit of 'padding' his words with responses to criticisms or reactions he anticipates coming from a listener:

> When I spoke about my challenge, because my partner was still and had no judgement, I started to talk with much more freedom. It liberated me from creating unnecessary 'paddings' or 'fillings' that I construct in my head to justify or protect myself from criticism or judgement. That freedom made me narrate events in a more purposeful way without baggage and the burden of judgement. It was powerful to hear my own story, different to the one I had constructed in my head.

What this eloquent statement (which was offered verbally to peers and then written up) shows is just how much of our workplace dialogue and conversations are usually full of 'fillers', such as remarks that anticipate the criticism of others, positioning oneself as already doing or knowing something. These fillers thus often get in the way of the speaker being clear, and are also part of a listener 'second-guessing'—deciding what they are hearing and how they feel about it, almost before it is said. When this student shared this experience with the class, many other students really heard it, and began noticing the impact of their own 'fillers' or 'paddings' in speaking and listening. For example, one student took the insight into a coaching exercise with a peer and later remarked, 'I felt I really tuned in—the questions I asked were more direct, without the "fill".'

As I described in the Introduction, many of these practices such as mindful listening are not new. When I have worked with groups of Indigenous leaders on listening, they frequently say, 'Oh but that's what our elders do and have done for generations.' Indeed, Indigenous cultures all over the world have strongly developed practices of silence and listening. *Dadirri* is an Aboriginal word describing an inner deep listening and a quiet, still awareness that encompasses the presence of an unspoken knowledge and authority.[3] As described by Indigenous author Judy Atkinson in her book *Trauma Trails*, leaders who practice *dadirri* enact:

- knowledge of community and respect for the diversity of individual contributions to it
- a non-intrusive observation and quietly aware watching
- deep listening, 'hearing with more than the ears'
- a reflective, non-judgemental consideration of what is being seen and heard
- having learned from listening, a plan for action informed by wisdom and the responsibility that comes with knowledge.

A final example about the value for leaders in listening mindfully comes from secondary schools. Many schools have embraced mindfulness as a tool to help students, especially at senior levels, cope with stress and develop resilience. There are also curriculums such as *MindUP* that help children from kindergarten or preparatory levels onwards to develop important capabilities in being able to relax, and put into perspective difficult or challenging experiences. My role has usually been to work with school leadership teams on how mindfulness can contribute to school leadership, creating empowering school cultures.

Like many organisations, schools are hectic, highly pressured and time-structured environments with established norms of listening and speaking. Teachers are more used to talking than listening, and they are expected to give advice and problem-solve. The first benefit of mindfulness is helping them see how some of these habits and routines may get in the way of the transformations they are after. Teachers know that the most sustainable solutions are the ones students find for themselves when supported to do so. Mindfulness thus encourages teachers to pause, notice and interrupt their usual speaking and listening habits. It helps them find a different place from which to listen to students: one that doesn't necessarily take more time but creates a space in which students feel held to find a new path themselves.

On the basis of his work with leaders in a wide range of contexts, Richard Searle says that deep, generous listening changes what is possible for others. He draws distinctions between listening *to*, listening *for*, and where we are listening *from*, suggesting that we can be much more useful as leaders by changing where we are listening from (see Figure 3: Levels of listening). For him, the power of mindful listening is that it creates a space for speakers themselves to generate new insights and possibilities. Simply through listening from stillness rather than telling, the first step is that individuals take responsibility for what's happened and what's going on now. Second, listening from stillness can encourage speakers to take responsibility for adapting and opening themselves to new insights and practices in the future. This extra step of helping people become more open to change is often a key role for leaders, and it may be more effectively accomplished by mindful listening than by telling.

Listening is one of those activities that are pervasive in leadership yet often done on automatic pilot with little positive effect. In his book *Quiet Leadership,* David Rock encourages leaders to listen for potential and possibility—what might be there.

Mindful listening suggests small and not time-consuming changes in the way we listen which can substantially shift others' experience of the world, their insight and sense of empowerment in tackling important issues. Collective mindful listening and dialogue, the subject of the next chapter, can also be a container for learning and creativity.

Seven

DIALOGUE FOR INSIGHT

Dialogue is about evoking insight.
William Isaacs

While talk is central to leadership work, the talk that prevails in most workplaces and organisations is unhelpful at best, deadening and disempowering at worst. Meetings are often interminable and achieve little; conversations are superficial, marooned on the tidal flats of jargon or unspoken feelings and resentments. How do leaders go beyond politeness, routinised exchanges and 'tuning out' in conversing? How do we make conversations matter?

Mindfulness is usually understood to be a solitary, internal activity. While this is partially true and the research discussed so far shows how mindfulness changes internal processes such as thinking and giving attention, mindfulness is also fundamentally an *inter*personal activity. In Buddhist traditions, the point of cultivating mindfulness is to benefit others. Happiness and fulfilment are not achieved in isolation but with, through and for others. For example, 'Engaged Buddhism' is advocated by Thich Nhat Hanh and other teachers to remind followers that the purpose of practice is social change to reduce suffering and oppression in the world. Meditators are urged to get off their cushions and enact their mindfulness practice in their interactions in the day-to-day world, not through silence but through skilful conversations, dialogue and action.

In my experience of working with mindfulness in groups of different kinds, the biggest impact on leadership occurs not just at the level of the individual practitioner but in interaction with others, through listening and conversation. Yet when I teach this material with groups, a first response is often, 'But there are times when you just have to tell people. That's what they want!' That is probably true. Equally, there are many myths about the value of telling and issuing orders in leadership. In many situations where there seems to be not much room or reason for listening or exchange, there is often still value in pausing and ensuring one's speaking is clear, focused and impactful, rather than reactive or with unintended consequences.

In my first job after university, I joined an Australian government semi-autonomous organisation, researching and planning large road and transport projects. It may not sound it, but it was a very engaging job where I learned a lot about organisations and how things happen in them. I worked in multidisciplinary teams composed of engineers, economists, planners, environmental scientists and others. 'The Bureau', as it was known, was well-funded and there was support to thoroughly investigate the social, environmental and public policy aspects of various road and community development projects. My job as a junior social scientist was typically to represent the voices of residents of inner city areas, environmental action groups and other stakeholders who might otherwise not be heard in the normal course of public policy-making.

Despite many aspects of the job being rewarding, my experience working in teams was not. The orthodoxy that was around in those days, and still is to a large degree, was that multidisciplinary, ideally 'self-managing' teams was the way to achieve better, more innovative and more binding decision-making and was preferred over traditional decision-making structures. Yet my own experience was the absence of dialogue. There was a well-understood hierarchy, of which I occupied the bottom. There was a lot of talk and argumentation but very little genuine listening. Being seen to offer expert opinion was key and admissions of ignorance or even ambivalence were out. Meetings were held and the illusion of discussion and consultation performed. But no real work was done at most of those team meetings or in the conversations that surrounded them.

I now know that working in and learning from groups doesn't have to be like this. In fact, in much of my MBA and executive development work, the dynamics of the group, their unfolding discussions and deepening capacities to hear and learn from each other are key influences which enable individuals to make important changes in their view of themselves, their behaviour and the challenges they are working on in leadership. In the rest of this chapter I share some of the insights from research and some practices that I have found helpful in promoting mindfulness in one-on-one conversations and in group or team meetings.

There are many reasons people are not present in conversations: perceived time pressure; attachment to predefined solutions and views of the problem; needing certainty; discomfort with different points of view and its polarising effects; ego attachment to the idea that the leader needs to be the one who knows, the expert. Many of us see conversations and meetings as opportunities to trade or withhold information, to earn points or credibility, and we can be encouraged by organisational norms to take this view.

While some of these obstacles can seem intractably embedded in identities and organisational habits, our own experience working with leaders is that introducing them to ways of being more mindful in interactions is actually quick and simple. They find it takes no extra time; in fact, it often enables conversations to be shorter because all parties are genuinely in the room, with a commitment to saying what is felt and real.

So what are some of the keys to help lead this shift? A first step, in both one-on-one conversations and group meetings, is pausing and noticing one's intent. In *Difficult Conversations*, Douglas Stone and his colleagues argue the key to shifting the tone and potential outcomes in difficult conversations is a shift in mindset from telling to learning (see Figure 4).

How do you help yourself and others make this shift from telling to learning something? Pausing before conversations and taking the time to remind ourselves of the overarching purpose and what might be helpful to the other person is a useful start. As described in the preceding chapter, another useful step is taking a moment to separate our own 'stuff'—our feelings of being pressured or irritated by some other matter. Mindfulness encourages us to draw on our bodies and breath, as well as our mind, in this process. Gregory Kramer's very useful book *Insight Dialogue* is based on the premise that meditation is as much an *interpersonal* practice, as an *intrapersonal* practice.[1] Kramer outlines six embodied steps that we might consciously initiate in order to be fully present and available to the other in conversation:

- Pause (mindfulness).
- Relax (acceptance): relax the body, drop the shoulders and the jaw.
- Open (spaciousness): take a deep breath, open across the chest.
- Trust emergence (letting go, letting come): be prepared to relinquish plans, invite and welcome whatever comes up.
- Listen deeply (receptivity).
- Speak the truth (integrity and care).

Although this is a model that comes from meditation, in my own work with leaders and students I sometimes take the time to introduce it and step people through it in an embodied way. There is often awkwardness and a bit of jocularity and resistance. However, my experience is that inviting the group to spend a few moments experiencing an embodied presence, before conversing, changes the feel of a group and influences the quality of the discussions that then occur.

In situations where leaders are using group conversation to solve problems or create new solutions, mindfulness and the capacity to offer our full presence to the task and each other is critical. A group of researchers aligned with Massachusetts Institute of Technology, including William Isaacs, Peter Senge and Otto Scharmer, following the work of physicist and student of thought David Bohm and others, have explored how to create the conditions for creative dialogue. Although there is extensive and often very good research on group and team dynamics, I have selected this work because the conditions it identifies for dialogue are also those offered by mindfulness.

According to Isaacs, groups often move through a series of 'fields' in conversation. Field 1, or Politeness, is where groups start and often spend most time. In this field, conversations are routinised and predictable, familiar norms are followed and

From	To
Intention of telling	Intention of learning something new
Stance of certainty	Stance of openness to the moment, curiosity
Focusing on what happened, who's right	Hearing and allowing for multiple interpretations of events
Feelings need to be suppressed	Attuned to feelings, providing important data

Figure 4: A shift from telling to dialogue
(Adapted from Stone et al. 2000)

agendas dealt with. But people don't say what they are feeling and thinking and no real work is done. In my doctoral research, politeness and routinisation was where most of the management teams stayed and it is also the field occupied, sometimes dangerously, by boards responsible for advice and governance.

In Field 2, Positionality, at last someone says something they believe. But a move towards more honest statements then often elicits exchanges where individuals defend positions and themselves: 'I am my point of view.' The resulting conflict and discomfort means teams often revert to politeness, with some group members feeling silenced and disenfranchised.

Isaacs argues that each of these stages is mediated by particular crises. If the group is prepared to slow down, suspend judgement and really listen, then two further fields become possible. In Field 3, Reflective Dialogue, there is the preparedness to be present to what's unfolding rather than push agendas. Group members notice and reflect on their own behaviour and 'what's going on' at a deeper group level. There is a temporary release of pressure to make a decision or all agree. There may be recognition that others have something to teach us. In Field 4, Generative Dialogue, the group loosens preconceptions of who they are and what they are trying to do together. A climate of trust and permissiveness allows both valuable creativity and play to become possible.

There is nothing inevitable about movement through these fields and there are undoubtedly situations where genuine group dialogue is not what's needed. However, our own experience is that groups are often quite stunned to see that they can, together, create an entirely different climate of openness, listening and learning, even after quite a short time together. A further powerful insight is that it doesn't take much more than a willingness to slow down, to notice, to be prepared to share responses rather than opinions, and to suspend judgements.

Significantly, you don't have to be the formal leader to shape dialogue in a group. Individuals can have impact by offering different kinds of responses and observations into the group space. They can help 'hold' the container for gradually larger sets of ideas, pressures and people as the different crisis points unfold.[2] Some MBA students and executives exposed to these practices go back to their regular meetings and try effectively 'being different'. One of my students was the most junior member of the executive team of a creative design and marketing organisation. He found that some quite small interventions on his part, requiring him to take risks and be vulnerable, unlocked an initially emotional, then incredibly useful, discussion of the organisation's strategic options.

A related body of research from Otto Scharmer and his colleagues explores how these same dynamics and a commitment to being present can foster innovation and allow for new futures to emerge. According to Scharmer's Theory U, groups can be supported to move from usual patterns of 'downloading' and 'reacting with quick fixes' to co-creating new futures. When faced with the opportunity to innovate, teams typically move through three mindsets in turn: judgement, cynicism and fear. Each of these mindsets are familiar ways in which groups defend against the need for change. For example, when I initiate a different class process, mode of teaching and set of expectations to a new MBA Leadership class, students consistently exhibit these three successive responses. It's valuable—though not always immediately welcome—to point out or help them notice the way these three 'voices' routinely cut in, shutting down new ideas and getting in the way of group learning.

Scharmer's view of the role of leadership in dialogue is not complex but guided by a spirit of experimentation. Leaders can:

- Hold the space by slowing down and listening to understand (not telling).

- Observe with mind open, suspending voices of judgement and cynicism.
- Tune to the senses, including connecting with the heart and (re)connecting with overarching intention/purpose.
- Design prototypes and pilot opportunities by integrating head, heart and hand.
- Access the 'whole cathedral' around one, not just the instrument to hand.

Distilling the research described above and experiences working with leaders, the following steps can help us foster mindfulness in conversations and dialogue:

1. Pause: this process need only be momentary, supported by relaxing the body and breathing consciously out. Recognise if our minds are in another place and then become present.
2. Remind ourselves of our overarching intent and the purpose of the conversation, and reflect on our own 'stuff' that we might be bringing and could let go of.
3. Open ourselves to be present and prepare to be influenced by what might unfold.
4. Commit to being real and honest, not polite or shallow.
5. Listen with more than the ears (see Chapter 6 'Listening from stillness').
6. Suspend judgement: as we listen, observe ourselves. Watch for certainty and premature attachment to certainty. Recognise there is a choice: to either form an opinion and align our identity behind it, or to not do so and remain open.
7. Experiment with sharing feelings and observations without being too attached to them.
8. Allow attention to broaden, tuning in to emotions and drawing on all the senses.

9. Ask questions but notice if our questions are really opinions or judgements in disguise. Everyone else will know if they are. Avoid giving answers, as doing so is rarely helpful in dialogue. The most powerful things to volunteer are usually feelings or observations.

10. Continue to observe and reflect-in-action about our own reactions (see Chapter 5 'Reflecting on identity with less ego'). Have we drifted off, are we waiting to offer a solution or to jump in with our own perspective?

11. Maintain compassion towards self, thus not beating ourselves up if things don't go as we hoped.

12. Appreciate and enjoy what unfolds, especially moments of clarity, statements that generate insight and support for others.

Eight

CONNECTING

*It is through connecting with other people, actually making
a difference to others and bringing joy into their lives,
that we make our own lives matter.*
Thupten Jinpa

Being prepared to connect with another is central to leadership. Connecting, in essence, means being present, in that moment, to that whole person. To be connected doesn't require a long-term relationship or the capacity to invest lots of time and energy in understanding. One of the most powerful and practical insights from mindfulness is that being present to someone else, even if just for a short time, can have quite profound impacts on them. They might feel deeply heard, held or empowered to try some new approaches. As a leader, being open to connecting with another involves making an active decision to set aside preconceptions, agendas and one's own needs. It is a rare and precious act. In this chapter I describe some of the different ways that mindfulness fosters connection with others, which in turn enables them to feel supported or empowered to take important steps.

About fifteen years ago I had a conversation with an eager and intelligent MBA student. He was in my leadership class and

I had just returned his first essay which was polished but on which I had given him a reasonable, but probably disappointing, grade. He was an enormously likable and able young man. I had written as part of my comments the suggestion that he come and discuss his essay with me, which he was now doing. In this meeting, as I do on many occasions and which most of us do, I faced a choice. I could have a routine discussion about the 'nuts and bolts' of how he could improve his essay and get a better mark for the next—a strong motivator for most MBA students. His demeanour when we met was respectful but my hunch was that, at that stage anyway, he wasn't allowing much to touch him—a demeanour that I come across often among managers and leaders who are driven.

The choice for me, and it is an 'in the moment' choice that we all make in day-to-day work, was whether to try to connect with some part of him that hadn't—to date—been available. How could I get his deeper attention? And in so doing, how could I get something from him that was very different and potentially of far more value (to him and the class) than what he was currently delivering? I said something like the following: 'You will succeed in this subject and likely be seen as a leader by doing as you are doing, but it will be a missed opportunity and potentially superficial. Or you can open yourself and risk putting more of yourself into the class and the work. I would really like to see you do the latter.'

Then about two years ago I was teaching one of the Williamson Leadership Program cohorts that I describe in Chapter 5 'Reflecting on identity with less ego'. The person who introduced me was that same MBA student. He described the impact that our short conversation had had on him. It wasn't the overall subject, it was most particularly the brief conversation itself that made the impact. It had set in train some big changes, many not immediately. He had changed careers and was now involved, very successfully and happily, in senior executive recruitment and selection. But the thing he focused on in his introduction of me to his Williamson Program cohort was how that conversation opened up the possibility for him of initiating—leading—a deeper and more honest relationship with his father. To the observer, this person might have come across as leading a highly successful life. He was, as I said, smart and accomplished in most things he took on. But he had suffered at a more personal level from never knowing his father and more broadly from keeping some relationships at arm's length, not voicing his deeper needs or feelings. He described that the most important outcome of our conversation was realising that he could authorise himself to initiate a more honest relationship with his father, having the courage to do something that neither he nor his father had been able to do. He managed to do this before his father had died of a protracted illness and not long before he introduced me on the Williamson Program.

I had a memory of him and of our conversation but we had virtually no contact since those days when he was an MBA student. I do remember that in that meeting with him about his essay, I made a conscious effort to be present and not have the easier, polite conversation but to express my belief in, and challenge to, him to deliver more than his usual accomplished but glossy front. I need to add here that there have been many other examples where, because of fear of repercussions (including students' evaluations of me and my subject!), I have gone the polite route with much less positive results. But there are a fair number of other occasions where, facing hostility from someone opposed to me and what they felt I was asking, making a connection turned around our relationship. What often transpired was that they had rarely, in a work or professional setting, had someone go below superficial exchanges to connect with them and invite their deeper engagement.

I want to provide this example because it reinforced to me how significant we can be to others when we offer our preparedness to be present, a core aspect of mindfulness. There likely were other things conspiring to encourage this MBA student to step up and take a risk with how he was being, especially with his father. The lesson for me, though, was that it didn't take much from me beyond making that choice to connect. It didn't take long. It just took for me to be present, without preconceptions, and to care about him, to show in my advice that I believed in him and could see something in him that currently was holding him back but that he could free up.

Connecting with, mentoring and supporting others often involve these elements of mindfulness: a commitment to be present and to be real and honest. As leaders we also need to have faith that the people with whom we are working often already know, at some level, that things need to change. Second, leaders need to trust that individuals have the insights and capacity to solve the challenges they face already *in* them. Our job is to help them find, or re-find, those new ways forward.

Do the same principles of mindful connecting apply in leadership coaching? The activity of coaching is a contested area in management and leadership. There are many approaches and techniques; for example, some that focus squarely on business performance outcomes, while others have a 'life coaching' orientation with personal goals. There is mixed evidence of coaching's effectiveness, depending on what one is measuring. Coaching sits alongside mentoring and sponsorship as activities that can support leaders to become more effective and fulfilled in their work. The distinction between these activities is potentially important. In the area of women's leadership, for example, there is strong evidence that to actually get women to be seen as eligible for senior positions, they often need sponsors, not mentors—that is, senior people who are prepared to put their name forward to employers, boards and recruiters, and then back them for jobs and opportunities.

In his book, *Mindful Leadership Coaching*, Manfred Kets de Vries draws on his long experience working as a coach to senior executives to identify aspects of mindfulness that are pivotal in coaching. For example, part of what good coaches do is use themselves as an instrument in the moment: to listen deeply and respectfully, to use their senses to know when to protect and nurture, and when to challenge, the individual they are coaching. Kets de Vries places a high value on connection, arguing that 'the kind of relationship that is established is the deciding factor in creating meaningful change'.[1] Building on neuroscientific research, he also emphasises the importance of encouraging executives to 'focus their attention on the sensations, feelings and thoughts they had not previously acknowledged'.[2] Without engaging the senses, the intuitive, spontaneous and emotional parts of the brain, any change that occurs will be an intellectual understanding of a dilemma that will almost certainly prove to be a transitory solution.[3]

I came to coaching accidentally, initially. Students and colleagues with experience of my leadership work began to recommend me to others who were seeking help to navigate a shift or hiatus in career—and sometimes in life. I don't have a coaching qualification and have always entered into these relationships being clear about the kinds of things I might offer and the processes we might follow. It is always preferable in my experience to have an open and emergent view of how useful one can be as a coach! What I do doesn't look like many forms of executive coaching; for example, we don't set goals and I don't use any diagnostics. I ensure there are opportunities to review and 'opt out' if the person I'm working with judges our conversations not useful. Having said this, there is often an ebb and flow over sessions, with some feeling a bit stuck and others more powerful. The coaching arrangements we make are, accordingly, sometimes open-ended and extend for many years or, at the other extreme, may be over a six- or nine-month period and are focused on supporting someone facing a specific challenge, such as moving to a new leadership role.

Coaching opportunities are sources of great learning for me—often the best parts of my role! As is often found in mentoring situations, a powerful direction of learning is the mentor learning from mentee, not the other way around. So it has been in my coaching work. The people I have worked with have taught me lots (and continue to do so)—not just about the idiosyncrasies of their sectors, organisations and stakeholders, but also the surprising delights and satisfactions of their work. It is inspiring and my learning from these coaching opportunities is threaded throughout this book.

Why is a preparedness to be present and connect a critical foundation of coaching? First, part of the challenge in coaching is that the presenting problem or pretext is rarely a useful guide to the real issue or obstacle. My main job is often simply to pause, and reinforce the value of giving time and attention to understanding what is going on or what is at the bottom of things for the person with whom I am working. Sometimes this is an emotional process and people apologise and say they feel awkward taking up my time on this, yet it is essential.

Generally people give a lot of clues almost immediately in the way they talk about leadership experiences or relate their stories. I often only need to hint at these clues in my observations for them to recognise underlying issues or obstacles for themselves. This is not therapy. It is about leadership and helping capable leaders give attention to both what is getting in the way for them and what will help them thrive and flourish as they go about their work.

Lesson number two is the need to get your ego out of the way in coaching. It's not about what you know or about problem-solving. People often present at coaching thinking that I am going to tell them what they need to do to change or to 'step up' to a new set of challenges. It is tempting, then, to think that the coaching task is to draw on one's own experience to suggest ways forward. Although this might sound helpful, and one can feel a lot of pressure to come up with solutions, my experience is that filling the space with strategies or solutions almost never is.

Lesson number three, then, is that to work effectively with someone or, more simply, to be helpful, we need to make a commitment to connect in a human, compassionate way. The infrastructure of coaching—diagnostics, action plans, incremental progress reviews—in my experience are sometimes ways of avoiding this human connection. Tools and instruments, such as 360-degree feedback, can be of value, but they shouldn't ever take the place of being genuinely there. Coaches are often under pressure by boards or employers to demonstrate the worth of their executive coaching work in bottomline terms. The challenge is to ensure these pressures don't undermine the main focus, which is to be present to the person you are with, as they are now, and to help them be as fulfilled and effective as they can be in their leadership. Occasionally this means supporting them to push back or speak out against organisational demands, and, more rarely, to leave current roles and pursue other leadership paths.

CONNECTING WIDER COMMUNITIES

The above examples are about how mindfulness can help us connect with others in direct and one-on-one interactions. But there is further evidence that practising mindfulness can build a sense of connection across wider communities. 'Mindful in May' is an online global meditation campaign, the creation of

Melbourne-based social entrepreneur Elise Bialylew. Bialylew came to mindfulness and meditation as a doctor specialising in treating psychiatric conditions in the public health sector. Seeking to manage her own work stresses as well as learn more holistic ways to support her patients, she attended a conference of leading researchers sharing their findings about the positive impact of mindfulness meditation on the brain. Recognising the potential to harness this practice in her own work, Bialylew decided to draw on social media and technology to create an accessible mindfulness platform to reach people around the world. She also saw an opportunity to inspire people to turn their attention to global issues and raise money to help make a difference to many living in developing countries unable to access clean water.

Since its conception, Mindful in May has seen thousands of people from around the world learning mindfulness skills online through the one-month program, which includes audio guided practices and expert interviews with some of the leading scientists and teachers in the field who inspired Elise's own journey and learning. In addition to the benefits received by the participants, thousands of people in developing countries have benefited through the funds raised to support water projects in Africa.

Schools, hospitals, government organisations and corporates have participated in Mindful in May and all share their surprise at the significant benefits of being supported through the program to commit to ten minutes of practice a day. Bialylew, was interested in answering the question: how much practice do you need to do in order to derive benefit?

'Anecdotally, I know that one month of ten minutes a day of mindfulness meditation has significant benefits for people ranging from improved sleep, reduced stress levels, a sense of greater appreciation in daily life—however as a scientist I wanted to research if this was a reliable, objective finding.'

Bialylew is in the process of researching the impact of the Mindful in May program on participants to provide an evidence-based answer to what 'dose' of mindfulness is the minimum required.[4]

For Bialylew, there is another form of cross-generational connection that underpins her own leadership. Her grandparents were Holocaust victims and refugees to Australia and her own early upbringing was not sheltered from understanding the full horror of those experiences. She remembers asking her mother as a child, how could people have stood by as these events unfolded. Her own career as a doctor and now social activist reflects a deep commitment to not stand by but to assist people in practical ways to work for change. Watching how Mindful in May has taken off as a global campaign, Bialylew notes that mindfulness is fundamentally a practice of care and compassion for oneself, which naturally extends out to others in our lives. It promotes a sense of interconnection for individuals who may otherwise feel estranged or dislocated from self, family or community. In Elise's experience, practicing mindfulness creates an opening of the heart, which supports a spirit of greater social responsibility and care for the well-being of fellow humans and the planet.

Mindful in May is one of a number of very successful online approaches and programs aimed at supporting people to become mindful. 'Smiling Mind' is another program that is being widely introduced in Australian schools, again using an app that simply leads students through a short meditation at the start of the day or a class. Extensive research is being gathered about the outcomes. What these experiences show is that 'online' need not necessarily mean disconnection from others. The possibilities are that not only will it help individual students focus and give better attention to their studies, but that it will also foster a sense of wider community and care for others.

Nine

BEING MINDFUL IN CRISES

*Better decisions don't necessarily flow from
more logical thinking.*
Malcolm Gladwell

What typically happens in a crisis for leaders? In the first few hours, in cognitive terms, there is often denial, shock or disbelief, followed by reactivity and then reversion to highly honed responses. There is enormous pressure on leaders at this stage to be directive and 'take charge', to act and look like one is in control.

In his research on public sector leadership, mindfulness researcher Paul Atkins identifies two alternative 'pathologies' when leaders respond to crises.[1] The first is over-differentiation, where seeing all the problems and the scale can lead to feeling overwhelmed and paralysis. The other is under-differentiation, where excessive certainty and rigidity can prompt pre-emptive interpretations and categorisations, followed by shutting down to new or emerging information.

At a senior level, there are also many cultural pressures on decision-makers which can lead to mindlessness, despite good intentions. Organisationally encouraged processes of conceptualisation, such as developing the categories and typologies core to consultants' intellectual property, can become tied up with identities. The reproduction and elaboration of such processes comes to be 'seen as reality, strength, permanence'.[2] For example, the constructions of invincibility which were seen in many banking cultures before and precipitating the 2007 global financial crisis are, from this perspective, symptoms of mindlessness. Equally, models of information processing often assume and demand logic and linearity in areas and phenomena laden with uncertainty. Leaders come under pressure to adopt heuristics which preserve illusions of predictability and accuracy where there may be little. In crises, these pressures on individual leaders become more pronounced. Good crisis leadership is about 'taking charge', doing and acting, not reflecting or consulting—or so the conventional wisdom goes.

Crises and difficult events elicit a cascade of physical and psychological effects in individuals, such as high levels of arousal and adrenalin, fear and 'flight and fight' responses, which in turn flow through into workplaces, organisational relationships and leadership.

Organisations, equally, exhibit structural responses to such events that impact information flows, distributions of power and decision-making.

While some of these interrelated individual and systemic reactions are supportive of good crisis or emergency leadership, others have been shown to exacerbate disasters, both in terms of immediate management and the longer, and sometimes tougher, post-crisis and prevention phases. A substantial body of research on crisis management exists, but in this chapter I focus on work that explores applications of mindfulness.

In leadership of crises the challenge is multi-faceted. First, leaders need to recognise the cognitive and attachment processes by which egos, cognitive routines and mindlessness get embedded. This recognition involves processes of reflection on, and in, action that were discussed in Chapter 5 'Reflecting on identity with less ego'. To pursue mindfulness can thus involve for the individual leader an attentiveness that is deeply 'counter' cultural.

For leaders seeking to remain mindful through crises, strategies can include:

- having mechanisms for staying open to advice and feedback, especially from outsiders and critics who sometimes get scapegoated during and after crises
- maintaining capacity to focus attention, but also learn 'on the run'
- routines for slowing down and stepping back to take stock and get perspective as the crisis unfolds
- being open to acknowledging feelings and working with emotion, even though shutting off feelings—one's own and others'—is attractive (see also Chapter 16 'Feeling').

CREATING ORGANISATIONAL MINDFULNESS

Can a 'culture' of mindfulness help organisations deal with crisis? At an organisational as well as individual level, research shows that an immediate reaction is often 'threat-rigidity'. Faced with an emergency, organisations tend to centralise power and decision-making and reduce their environmental scanning and diverse mechanisms of information processing. This can, in turn, reduce capacity to give attention to diverse aspects of the unfolding situation, notice the unexpected or communicate openly with affected stakeholders.

Organisational life and organising, by their very nature, often elicit default mindlessness. Routines, procedures, heuristics and developed 'logics' of problem-solving are often aimed at removing discretion and room for error. Organisational researchers, such as Karl Weick and his colleagues, draw on psychological theories and definitions of mindfulness, particularly the work of psychologist Ellen Langer, to apply in their analyses of organisational systems under conditions of failure.[3] They define organisational *mindlessness* as including symptoms such as relying on past categories, acting on 'autopilot', minimising attention for new information, and fixating on a single perspective. Cruelly, as 'safety cultures' get more normalised and ingrained (with, for example, work shifts commencing with 'tick-the-box' audits), the risk is that people 'check out', become more mindless, and fail to notice important changes in environment or circumstance. The same processes that are designed to minimise disasters can thus make them more 'normal' or likely.[4]

In their research on High Reliability Organisations, Weick and his co-researchers argue that mindful features can be made part of the culture of organisations—widespread and common but not institutionalised—thereby maintaining their everyday power to invite mindfulness. Some of these organisationally embedded features of mindfulness include:

- close attention and sensitivity to operations and processes
- reluctance to simplify and categorise observed phenomena, rather giving attention to the particular here and now
- commitment to resilience or a culture which values investigation and learning
- 'preoccupation' with failure, meaning an interest in failure and learning from it, rather than avoiding or brushing it under the carpet
- underspecified decision structures; that is, decision-making that is not overly hierarchical with the expectation that discretion will be used by people at different levels.

Seeking to cultivate collective mindfulness and to lead by example, as demonstrated in research and case studies, can have many benefits for navigating organisational change and innovation. Giving attention to particular circumstances and context can help executive teams avoid 'groupthink' or the 'bandwagon effect'.[5] For example, in their study of US health care in the late 1990s, researchers C. Marlena Fiol and Edward O'Connor show that hospitals which delivered high quality services and increased their market share were those that mindfully resisted the 'bandwagon' solution which swept the industry and argued that the only way to survive was integration, amalgamation and economies of scale. Other organisations, often led by people with a commitment to mindfulness, embed principles of focused attention and compassion in the way they operate. Research suggests that these organisations can experience a kind of 'bandwagon-proofing' because their way of operating is tied to underlying values and less susceptible to market fads.

RE-PERCEIVING

From both Buddhist philosophy and neuroscientific research on thinking and stress comes the knowledge that while difficult events occur, what is often more important to our lives, resilience and ongoing well-being is how our minds construct, interpret and make sense of those events. At times when I have felt hopeless or in the midst of a terrible failure, it has been very helpful to me to be reminded that the source of at least some of the pain is not the particular circumstances but my mind's machinations about them, including all the self-judgement, shame or regret that may be part of that thinking. This is not to say that bad and painful things don't happen, and that sadness and grief aren't appropriate responses to them. It is just that we have some choice in what we make of them.

This is, of course, the great insight from those who have experienced unimaginable horrors such as the Holocaust, the Cambodian genocide or the Chinese invasion of Tibet. Terrible experiences teach us sharply about life and its value, and it's often people who have experienced horror who are the most compelling advocates for living fully and compassionately. Listening to Thich Nhat Hanh describe his experiences of the war in Vietnam, where his team of social workers were being massacred by both sides of the conflict, his story is one of finding compassion for the soldiers, ordered to do such terrible things.

Knowing that we have influence over how difficult times affect us will assist in gaining perspective and remaining resilient. I remember after a particularly disastrous teaching experience that haunted me for what felt like years, I realised that, eventually, it was just my thoughts that were inflicting so much misery. I had done the learning that needed to be done from that experience. I could now let the residual thoughts go. I'd thought them enough. What a relief! Similarly, in their work teaching mindfulness to stressed school and university students, academics Craig Hassed and Richard Chambers describe the freedom for students in realising 'I don't have to think that thought any more'.

At a broader societal level, the work of researchers such as Paul t'Hart shows that difficult times are often opportunities for leaders.[6] In crises, leaders play a key role in shaping community responses. Societies take their clues from leaders about when and where threat lies. As in the case of 'Weapons of Mass Destruction' (which turned out to be illusory or at least partially manufactured) that blighted Western and Middle Eastern nations through 2001 to 2003 and led to the invasion of Iraq, threats are always appraisals of what is happening, not objective reality.

Thus, how societies respond to difficult times is very much dependent on the interpretations that are offered. As political scholar Joanne Ciulla shows, in distress we turn to authority, but leadership needs to help followers move beyond dependency or disempowerment. Communities can find the confidence to be resilient, to come together and make change. Crises can provide leverage to face up to and address moribund systems. They give political and community permission and authority to act. But as Paul t' Hart's extensive research warns, such responses require from leaders a suite of capabilities that are not necessarily rewarded in the heat of the moment.

The myth is that what makes a difference in crisis is the decisiveness and strength of the leader. The evidence is that an effective crisis response involves creating dynamic collaborations and decentralised networks. Accordingly, leaders need a commitment to staying open to the unfolding present, to giving attention to diverse data sources, separating data from interpretation, and what's real and solid from what are reactive and defensive thought processes. They need to remain committed to building individual and collective learning rather than just problem-solving or dealing with immediate burning issues.

Mindfulness is based on the understanding that we do not simply observe and react to the world. We actively create our own experience through the way we sense, interpret and make meaning and learning out of stimuli. Giving attention to the present unfolding moment, being able to discern new and important information among a flood of thoughts and interpretations, and focusing on the big picture of what needs to emerge out of crises are all qualities that mindfulness fosters. By cultivating individual mindfulness and working to build collective mindfulness, leaders may countervail some of the common responses to difficult circumstances and crises described in this chapter. Perhaps even more powerfully, mindfulness can help us think differently about the opportunities for change that can sometimes be mobilised from difficult times.

Ten

TRANSFORMING WRITING

I write from feeling, above all.
Richard Flanagan

While writing might seem to be less of a leadership concern and more an academic one, I want to suggest that writing matters for leaders. More and more of us are seeking to influence thinking (and therefore do leadership) by writing blogs and webpages, even crafting Facebook and brand identities. I am at work at that now! Yet with so much writing going on, its potential power has been masked. To write mindfully means writing with the reader in mind rather than telling. Writing has the capacity to change things for readers, to help see with fresh eyes, to re-know a phenomenon we thought we understood.

Why has writing been devalued? An awful lot of academic writing is truly indigestible for all but the narrowest in-group experts. Unfortunately, academics and educators often write in ways that install themselves at the top of hierarchies of knowledge, rather than to empower readers and students to find out for themselves.[1] Equally, popular business writing about leadership often comprises 'death sentences'.[2] Heaping banality and jargon on cliché, this kind of writing can kill stone-dead surprise, humour or delight.

Yet between, or perhaps completely outside, these two extremes is writing that has a different, more mindful relationship to the reader. Here, the author is not trying to beat the reader over the head or win them over to a particular view, not trying to sell or preach. Good writing is undertaken with the interests of the reader in mind but is often disruptive. It doesn't assume the reader is a dummy that has to have things spelt out in bullet point lists or three powerpoint slides. What does the latter do? It precludes the reader's involvement. It over-specifies and acts as if the reader's reaction is not part of the transaction. It seems to shout, 'This is what you need to think about this!'

To write mindfully, on the other hand, is to pause and ask why one is writing and who it is for. It invites us to set aside our own desire to tell and consider how a reader might like to encounter an understanding or idea. All great writing impacts at an emotional level as much as a cognitive one. You may be thinking to yourself that this is not relevant in business contexts where the point of the writing is to transfer information or convey instruction. Yet if we look closely, even in these specific contexts, information and instruction transfer are never just factual, they are always intended to have a particular impact on the receiver's understanding or actions. Even the best instructions may be experienced by readers as dictatorial, unnecessary or out of touch with the actual situation and therefore not relevant. In writing with the reader in mind, there is a lighter touch, informed by the view that the reader will take the seeds of what is useful or intriguing for them—without overstating the power and control by the author. These are all things I associate with mindfulness.

I was introduced to the French sixteenth-century philosophy of Michel de Montaigne by my daughter, Amy. Amy is doing her doctorate on early modern women's writing in Europe, focusing on Italian women of the sixteenth century. Amy's work has shown me just how innovative and radical authors of these periods were, especially some of the women. Bound tightly by complex codes of who was allowed to write, about what and how, some writers exhibited dazzling ingenuity in the way they communicated, engaged with readers and disrupted expectations. They experimented with their own identity as authors, refusing to allow others to 'pigeonhole' them or their message. Such stereotyping was one of the customary ways these women's hard-won power was diluted and their views neutralised. Many women writers cleverly and simultaneously reproduced (thus earning credibility and guaranteeing they would be read) and challenged authoritative writing. They changed the spaces and discourses about women's place through *the way they wrote*, not just what they wrote about.

Michel de Montaigne was a French landowner, born in 1533 in the Bordeaux region, who also turned writing and philosophical conventions on their heads. He was a leader in his own time, studying law and being appointed as a magistrate, inheriting and running a large estate near Bordeaux, then retiring at quite a young age after a near-death riding accident to write. The word 'essay' comes from Montaigne's work and the French verb *essayer*—to try. Thus, it was Montaigne who pioneered the essay: writing short 'tries' or explorations of aspects of experience that did not purport to be the truth or to be comprehensive.[3]

Most writers and philosophers of his time emulated the great classicists, producing writing that followed stylised prescriptive norms and never allowed the writer's own persona or frailties to be sensed. While Montaigne did some of this, he did it around and through the mundane and the personal, such as his relationship with his cat. In both how he writes his 'attempts at an answer' and the content of the ideas, Montaigne provides a revolutionary model for living and writing. He doesn't preach or prescribe, he reveals the complexity, his own shifts of heart and mind, but he has no agenda to make a compelling argument or convince the reader of the veracity of his views. In declaring 'I cannot keep my subject still', Montaigne pioneers new possibilities for writers and for readers, initiating stream-of-consciousness writing and modern literary understandings of readers as active participants in the creation of meaning.[4] Even more radically, he finds his subject matter in the ordinary day-to-day. He writes about thumbs, and how the mind hinders itself, on smells and on friendship.

Despite living centuries ago, Montaigne's explorations about how to live and lead are startlingly contemporary and mindful. For example, in author Sarah Bakewell's list of twenty of Montaigne's 'attempts' to answer 'how to live' are:

- don't worry about death
- pay attention to what is happening now
- read widely but slowly, forget or let go of a lot of what people tell you
- question
- be convivial, live with and enjoy others
- wake from the sleep of habit
- do a good job but don't get caught up in it
- give up control
- be ordinary and imperfect
- let life be its own answer.[5]

The reasons why Montaigne is so refreshing are many. I love the idea that writing does not have to claim to have answers, especially works of philosophy. Leaders might have much to learn from such notionally unsettling possibilities; that is, that we might be most useful to others by offering our own experiences in a direct and honest way and giving up personal agendas of persuading.

Just before I leave this part of the book, I want to mention another contemporary writer who provides a wonderful model of transforming writing. Thich Nhat Hanh is a Buddhist writer whose work I have read and profoundly benefitted from over many years. I draw on it throughout this book. His writing is entirely simple and direct. What comes through is that he has the reader's happiness and peace in mind. It imparts to the reader confidence to try simple things, to find new meaning in the profundity of life.

PART TWO

LEADING WITH BODY

Leadership has historically been portrayed as a cognitive and disembodied affair. If bodies rate a mention, it is usually about the problems they pose, how to manage body image or combat the physiological symptoms of stress. In this second part of the book I draw on examples and evidence to suggest that bodies, our breath and senses are gateways to finding presence and pleasure in leadership. Far from suggesting we need to suppress or control these aspects as part of doing leadership, I suggest ways they can support leaders to enjoy, even relish, their leadership work.

Sometimes when people think about mindfulness, they also think of it as some very elevated state where we are floating at a distance from the material world. But many Buddhist and other scholars argue that the separation of mind and body is a false and unhelpful dichotomy. Thich Nhat Hanh says that the way we get in touch with mindfulness and experience it is through the body and the breath.[1] There is also the common idea that to be mindful is to be self-disciplined, ascetically rejecting of the body, its needs and pleasures. I want to challenge this view.

Further, and although quite a lot has been written by leadership researchers about the importance of presence,[2] it is sometimes treated as an above-the-neck kind of phenomena. In contrast are a few leadership researchers who have tried to bring the body and physicality more 'front and centre' in understanding effective leadership. They show that good leadership is embodied and often has aesthetic qualities—it's part of what makes some leaders inspiring or engaging. One of these leadership researchers who brings to her work her own background in music and working with orchestras, Donna Ladkin, defines presence as an ability to shift the gaze away from future goals and outcomes, to being present to moments as they occur within the enterprise.[3] Ladkin is encouraging us to make the move from valuing leaders for their visions of the future to whether they are wholly with us here and now.

Very often in my work with leaders, I hear about a lot of suffering and pain. While many leaders say that their challenges—such as working very long hours, sacrificing family and relaxation for the job, spending energy 'executing' and inflicting difficult changes on people—just come with the territory, my own view is that leadership is potentially full of pleasure. It can be sensuous, delightful and joyful. Many of the most important experiences we have as followers as well as leaders are powerful because they have an embodied, sensual or pleasurable component, registered and valuable in our physical lives, not just in the mind. Such experiences help us to be resilient, cope with stress and find fulfilment in our work. In some of my other research and writing I have argued that the way leadership scholarship has developed—including the backgrounds and predilections of the scholars and practitioners who have largely written it—has skewed our understanding of what it is about and what we might offer in, and through, leadership.

This part of the book thus explores some controversial ideas about leadership and leading mindfully. A number of these ideas, such as being embodied and exploring eros, I have been writing about and testing with different leaders for some time. Others are newer. Either way, my intent is to help you delve into 'the cathedral' that is you. I invite you to experiment with how these other dimensions of you and your experience might allow for more presence and pleasure in your leadership.

Eleven

BREATHING CONSCIOUSLY

To know me is to breathe with me.
To breathe with me is to listen deeply.
To listen deeply is to connect.
Miriam Rose Ungunmerr-Baumann

Why might those involved in leadership pay attention to breathing? Breathing consciously is perhaps the simplest means through which leaders can become present and mindful. In this chapter, I describe both personal experience and a small number of research studies showing how watching and working with the breath can change outcomes for leaders and the people working with them.

But inviting leaders to notice or work with breathing in itself sometimes takes courage. It can be met with derision: 'I already breathe!' they joke. Or annoyance: 'I haven't got time for this!' Or even with an aggravated edge: 'I didn't pay (the thousands of dollars this course cost) to be told to breathe.' Exceptions might include those who have had training as musicians, singers or martial artists, who know that there are different ways to breathe and that these differences have significant consequences for one's performance. Typically, though, even people with this breath training haven't connected what they know about breathing to their leadership.

In a chapter of my book *Leadership for the Disillusioned* entitled 'Breath and mindfulness', I described some of my early, naïve and sometimes disastrous efforts to convey the potential impact of breathing to various groups of MBA students and executives that I was teaching. I had returned from completing my yoga teacher training a bit of a zealot. I was keen to make space for the groups I was teaching to step off the fast-track of their punishing schedules. I was keen to encourage them to pause, reflect and ask themselves how they wanted to be as leaders, rather than conforming to an organisational mould. Among the many lessons I learned from these experiences was that insisting people slow down and breathe consciously may be experienced as coercive! Inviting them to do so may be more skilful but is equally potentially confronting. Why is this so?

My experience is that breathing consciously is a difficult thing for some of us to do because it can highlight that we are not breathing much. Instead, we are holding our breath—to get through things, to ward off difficulties and feelings, to hold at bay or avoid facing what is happening in our lives. Our breath may be very shallow because we're running—fast. Vietnamese Buddhist monk and writer Thich Nhat Hanh says that we are conditioned to the habit of running because we think happiness lies in the future. I've heard myself say to me often, 'I'll just get through this next six months/project/program/reporting period/implementation and then I'll be able to enjoy life!' People I share this with often laugh in response as they recognise a similar mindset in themselves. 'Have you been reading my mind?' they ask. So, it is not until we give ourselves a moment to stop and take a conscious breath that it becomes possible to experience happiness now. Yet that step, in my experience, can be a deeply emotional one because it reveals just how hard we've been running and how much we have been deferring life and the possibilities of happiness.

Although part of this chapter explores evidence and research, breathing is one of those areas of mindfulness that is better if we simply experiment with it; for example, by stopping and noticing our own breath. If I have a message in this chapter, it is this: In your leadership work, when you are trying to influence others, wanting to take difficult steps yourself, or trying to support others to do new things, pay attention to the breathing patterns of yourself and others. Try pausing and deepening your breathing and see the effects on your mind's capacity to be aware and attentive.

WIDER RESEARCH ON THE BREATH

Many areas of artistic, creative, philosophical, yogic and martial arts traditions have well-developed understandings of the importance of breathing to our capacity to feel energised, to perform with presence, to convey emotion and impact, and to control thought. For example, in my yoga teacher training, which was located within the Himalayan tradition *svarodaya*, the science of breath was taught as the key to mind control. Swami Rama, a key figure in our teaching lineage, says, 'Controlling the breath is a pre-requisite to controlling the mind and the body.'[1] In yoga there are many breath techniques, such as *nadi shodanam*, or alternate nostril breathing, *kapala bhati* and *bastrika* practices which involve sustained periods of fast forced exhalations from the abdomen, to more challenging techniques of *kumbhaka*, or breath retention. Breath practices are designed to bring under conscious control the management of subtle energy flows known in yoga as *prana*, and in other traditions *chi* or *ki*. Studies have shown how yoga masters can indeed exercise, through their breathing techniques, extraordinary levels of energy and body control such as dramatically reducing nutritional needs and their heart rate. Although some of these feats, such as simulating death, are sensationalised in accounts, the ultimate aim of breath mastery is mind control.

Similarly in Buddhism, focusing on the breath is regarded as among the most reliable ways to develop mindfulness. Well over 2000 years ago the Buddha is recorded as teaching a sutra 'On the full awareness of breathing'. According to Thich Nhat Hanh's translation of and commentary on this teaching, the Buddha said: 'The method of being fully aware of breathing, if developed and practiced continuously, will have great rewards and bring great advantages.'[2] According to this ancient teaching, breathing with awareness can lead to awakening and liberation of the mind. If this sounds far-fetched and beyond the mundane realms of most of us, the Buddha's instructions are simple and practical. They basically amount to: 'Breathe in—notice you are breathing in; breathe out—notice you are breathing out. Keep practising.'

In his recent writing, such as *Peace of Mind*, Thich Nhat Hanh reminds us that even the most adept and experienced meditators might come back to the elemental practices of watching the breath. Consciousness is not much use to us, he says, if we are 'tossed around mindlessly like a bottle slapped here and there on the waves'.[3] Rather, our efforts to take hold of consciousness are made possible through the physical, most commonly through a focus on the breath. He instructs, 'Whenever mind becomes scattered, use breath as the means to take hold of mind.'[4]

Turning to situations of leadership and influence, one of the most powerful things my own yoga teacher, Jean-Alain D'Argent, showed me was that, as a teacher, one can encourage states in others through one's breath. Breathe out audibly towards the end of a shoulder rotation and students also breathe out, let go and release. Take a deep breath into the belly and let the diaphragm stretch out and down and others also breathe more expansively. Instructing a yoga class in an *asana*, such as a forward bend, for most of us leads to tightening or tension in the leg or hip muscles and joints. I often add the suggestion to 'Take your focus to muscles that are tight such as the hamstrings—breathe into them and feel that, especially on the exhale, you can relax and soften those muscles'. For many yoga students, taking the breath to a part of the body that's tight in this way, consciously exhaling and releasing that tightness, enables them to bring more movement or less rigidity and resistance.

Thus one's intentions as a teacher can be given physical expression through the breath. A way to influence the energy of others is to model a way of breathing oneself. To teach relaxation, you allow your own breath to slow and move to the stomach. In teaching meditation one's own breath becomes fine and delicate. Conversely, in an *ashtanga* yoga class, teachers use a *ujayi* breath (reducing the breath to a fine, slightly audible stream by partially closing the glottis or throat muscles). This breath is essential to enable focused attention and invigoration through a long, energetically demanding sequence of movements. In many forms of martial arts training, teachers similarly instruct in discipline, self-control and the targeted impact of moves often without words, rather through breathing. Students sense shifts in grounding, power and momentum through the teacher's breathing, and they learn how to reproduce these.

LEADING THROUGH CONSCIOUS BREATHING

Turning to more formal leadership theorising, research on the breath is still in its infancy.[5] However, a fascinating longitudinal study of leaders working with mindfulness was undertaken as part of doctoral research by an American scholar, Steve

Romano.[6] Romano was interested in examining how several specific practices introduced to leaders—including noticing and working with the breath, listening deeply, suspending judgement, fostering openness and expanded perspective-taking—would impact leadership abilities and, in turn, various leadership outcomes. The research mapped these effects over a 10–12 week period with a sample of six participants, all of whom were involved in leadership and management work. The results were self-reported but included improvements in capacity to take perspective, to think strategically and less reactively, to manage change and ambiguity in their roles, to listen and be patient with staff members, and to exhibit composure and avoid becoming defensive.

Romano's study—although using a small sample—was ambitious. It combined a range of training and coaching interventions with a series of scales administered over time and measuring outcomes such as experienced stress, mindfulness and other states. Among many interesting findings, most notable for our purposes in this chapter was the value to leaders of being taught breathing techniques. According to participants it was their capacity to tune into and change their breath that was both simple and effective at changing how they experienced work and its challenges. Attention to their breath elicited clear decreases in experienced body stress—no less than 'a life changer' according to some. Romano's results showed there was a lag between understanding breath practices cognitively and experiencing its results. He also suggests that breath awareness has these effects through three mediating mechanisms: it changes our relationship to self; it changes our relationships to others; and it brings us into the present, putting a value on the moment unfolding now.

Taking another perspective and in many Eastern philosophies and martial arts traditions, breathing is associated with building life energy, known as *chi* or *prana*. The purpose of disciplined practice in these traditions is not to become lithe but to build *prana* or *chi*, an inner centred-ness and vitality. That life force may be experienced in relationships by others as a grounded-ness, an authenticity or dynamism that a leader or teacher brings.

But breathing matters also in much more mundane settings, such as meetings, where relationships are being negotiated and leadership and influence attempted. Leadership scholar Donna Ladkin describes her coaching work with a senior accountant who had moved into a leadership role and, despite being respected as an expert, was suffering in his role, dreading team meetings, feeling as though he had to 'be' a certain way, and experiencing insomnia, anxiety and other physical and psychological symptoms as a result. The first thing to note is that in her diagnosis, Ladkin gave as much attention to this manager's physicality—his shallow breath, rushed and soft speech and hunched posture—as to his verbal description of his predicament and why he had sought help. Giving attention to these bodily symptoms encouraged her to take a non-conventional and tender approach to coaching, she could so feel his suffering.

Ladkin then set about taking a 'breath and body-based approach'[7] with this manager, where she instructed him in a variety of light stretches then diaphragmatic and abdominal breathing practices, helping him notice his breath and take the time, in the moment, to breathe more deeply, to exhale more fully, and in so doing relax and feel able to let go. In conjunction with some verbal coaching, the key changes that the manager noted in his day-to-day leadership work from breathing differently were:

- Time slowed down, he felt more in charge of and less pressured by time.
- With a slowing of time and a greater feeling of control over it, things fell into perspective and his priorities and overall purpose felt clearer.

- He was both more able to get in touch with his feelings and be less at their behest.
- He noticed how others were breathing, including a staff member, and recognising and tuning into their breath helped him to understand and feel empathy for them rather than simply seeing them as uncooperative and an obstacle as he had done before. He initiated a more open conversation with this person, his relationship with them improved, and he stopped agonising about and taking so personally the roadblocks they encountered together.

Romano also found his participants regarded this kind of help in slowing down and noticing the breath as simple but direct and uncontrived. This experience mirrors the Buddhist teaching that simply watching the breath changes things.

CASE NOTES FROM COACHING WITH A FOCUS ON BREATH

While the focus in coaching leaders is typically about working with goals, places they want to get to and changes they want to make, in my own coaching work, sometimes the most important place to be is helping individuals pause and notice where they are now. As discussed earlier in Chapter 8 'Connecting', workplaces and fast-paced lives can construct defences to doing this—they keep us running. But I know, and at some level the people know, too, that they can't keep going, they can't realise any goals, without giving themselves space to stop. In some cases, this is often why they find their way to coaching.

So, as part of our coaching relationship I will notice breathing and sometimes ask them to begin noticing it, too. The following are three examples:

Case 1: A very 'on the ball', smart individual is prone to jumping in quickly in conversations and group settings. His comments are well-intended but they don't have the effect he is looking for, which is to earn the respect of the group and have influence over emerging understandings. In a one-on-one with me, I point out how he is *being* in response to me—fast, not listening very well, on the edge of his seat, possibly holding his breath until he can 'jump in'. I also suggest he think about how others in the group might be reading his approach: for example, that he can barely wait for them to finish, that they cannot have anything to add, that their contributions are being tolerated but not really heard. I invite him to experiment with breath, pausing and reflecting on his seated position and his posture.

Case 2: A woman presents with a very controlled demeanour. She feels at risk of being overwhelmed by her emotion and exhibits a strong desire to bring feelings under control. We work on using the breath to allow emotion to just be there, to encourage her to experience that she doesn't have to work hard to drive it away. Breathing to trust herself to just be, to not feel she must change herself or change others. It takes a few months' work together but staying with this focus on the breath and acknowledging feelings starts to release her and she finds herself feeling lighter and freer, more able to be herself.

Case 3: A senior law firm partner who was previously a singer and chorister knew about breathing but didn't apply it in the potentially stressful presentation and facilitation roles she was often in. The 'homework' I set her was encouraging her to breath more consciously, allowing her pre-existing breath 'intelligence' and awareness to guide and ground her.

Wider research suggests that, beyond benefits to leaders themselves, the impact of being mindful of breathing is felt by others. Some therapists are trained to notice the breathing of those they are counselling. Adapting and modifying their own breath—for example, by slowing down and deepening, or by mirroring their client's breathing patterns—can help the people they are working with feel comfortable to relax and open. If the therapist signals with breath that now matters and there is time to listen, the collective or shared breath provides a container for new kinds of work to be done.

These studies confirm that registering how we are breathing and adapting the way we breathe are small adjustments that potentially have significant impact in leadership. There are sometimes situations where leaders can't do much. Difficult circumstances may leave few actions available and words may offer bare comfort. When we can't do much else, we can at least breathe consciously and, in so doing, be present with others. In less trying times, breathing consciously improves awareness of self and others, it helps us gain perspective on 'what's going on' and it reduces the stress we feel. As Ladkin points out, this can be done in any time or place and so is 'completely practical and do-able'.[8] Yet in an even more profound way, bringing consciousness of breathing into one's own leadership can help open oneself and others up to life. It reminds us all to notice and appreciate what life is offering: the relationships right here and the sensual possibilities of being alive.

Twelve

LOOKING AFTER BODIES

When we speak with our lives and our bodies we can
be very effective at changing the world,
whatever form this action takes.
Thich Nhat Hanh

I first began noticing the impact of bodies and an imposing physical presence in leadership due to my own particular short-comings in that department. More than once, leaders and students of leadership have contacted me, keen to meet and talk about my work, which had influenced them in some positive way or another. When some met me they couldn't stop themselves blurting out something like, 'But you're so small!' and then go on to add hurriedly, 'Never mind, you project big!'

I wasn't necessarily consoled by this reaction. It underlined clearly for me that while societies expect that leaders will be tall, imposing or charismatic, we don't own up to this expec-tation—it's often unspoken. This is despite the evidence of studies showing that, if you are a Western male manager, you are much more likely to be appointed to leadership—and to be paid more—if you are more than 6 feet tall. In *Blink,* Malcolm Gladwell describes this as the 'Warren Harding Error' or the tendency to impute leadership to 'tall, dark and handsome men'. Western societies accord leadership to men who fit such a profile, even if, as in the case of American president Warren Harding, he never once demonstrated leadership qualities or abilities.[1]

Perpetuated in much leadership theory there is a myth that the bodies of leaders and their followers are irrelevant. In this chapter I explore the idea that bodies and physicality *are* powerful allies in leading mindfully. I'm not suggesting that we all need to try to emulate the tall, masculine stereotype of leadership, but rather that our bodily experiences help us get out of our heads and be present to what's happening now. Our sense of physicality helps us literally 'step up' and be courageous, giving voice to issues or things we believe in. Even more powerfully, bodies and their evolutions connect us to others in our frailty, common humanity and mortality. One of the primary reasons people take on leadership roles is to improve the flourishing and well-being of others. At the bottom of it, this is what many leaders are on about, whether they are operating in educational, health, community, financial or customer service settings. As I seek to show with examples and evidence, an important part of delivering these leadership outcomes includes attending to, and looking after, our own and others' bodies.

MYTHS ABOUT BODIES AND PHYSICALITY IN LEADERSHIP

The myth that bodies are irrelevant in leadership has been fuelled from a number of directions. The authors of most leadership theory have historically been greying white blokes who've never had to notice the impact of bodies, or whose own bodies have been unproblematic for them for much of their lives. There are also those—and I put many of my fellow academics in this category—who have a whole history vested in the superiority of minds over bodies.

The myth is an understandable response for those among us who *want* bodies to be less relevant in leadership. This includes all those women and men of varied physical abilities, of different racial and cultural backgrounds, who don't 'fit' the template of physical attractiveness that societies and organisations recognise as 'leadership material'. When we choose leaders, it should be experience and capabilities that matter, not what we look like— but study after study has shown that bodies and attractiveness, or otherwise, are often implicit in judgements of leadership ability.

This is particularly the case for women leaders.[2] My own and other research has demonstrated that a vicious cycle occurs where women experience higher scrutiny of their bodies in leadership. They are told they must worry about how they appear—choosing a careful wardrobe and refining their media skills, not looking too ambitious or self-serving. Yet they are also told they mustn't look like they are worrying about how they look! If so, they are typically judged vain or self-absorbed. Several experiments have demonstrated the gendered norms at play in judging leadership. A Harvard study, for example, gave young men and women entrepreneurs identical 'pitches' to make to potential investors. The women were judged less deserving of financial support than the men and, if they were attractive, they encountered a further penalty—likely as having got to where they were because of their looks. In contrast, attractiveness in men was an asset—attractive men were judged as most likely to succeed.

One, not uncommon, response to this comprehensive (and not improving) evidence is to insist, and act as if, bodies don't matter in leadership. Yet I argue in this chapter and throughout this book that the separation in much of leadership theory between mind and body is deeply unhelpful to those interested in leading mindfully. To lead with mindfulness does not mean to ignore the body. Rather, the body is integrally connected to the mind. It is a source of valuable information about us and others, often made available to us in ways not registered in the conscious mind.

WHY PAY ATTENTION TO BODIES AS PART OF LEADERSHIP?

The value of being present—taking the trouble to physically 'be there'—is a central plank of leadership. It's been enshrined in the idea of MBWA (Management by Walking Around) and the decision that many new and long-standing leaders make to systematically and regularly visit and talk to employees and clients in even very large and geographically dispersed organisations.

Why is it so important for leaders to 'show up' in the flesh? First, it says that people matter and taking time to hear about their experiences and issues is a priority—at least as important as demanding board members or mountains of emails. Second, it signals courage and a willingness to literally stand before others as one is, without the protections of staff, minders, or corner offices in inaccessible and security-protected top floors. In this sense, being there in body is a political, democratising action for leaders.

I have written elsewhere about Christine Nixon, former Victorian Chief Police Commissioner and Chair of the Victorian Bushfire Reconstruction and Recovery Authority.[3] My ongoing work with Christine has taught me many important things about leadership. However, perhaps the most significant has been her preparedness—even when it was frightening and dangerous, confronting and traumatic—to go to places where affected people were, and listen. I had worked with previous police commissioners in Victoria and a more common response, especially in troubled organisations, is to give priority to political stakeholders, boards and strategic tasks, to get through the huge workload and, effectively, to hide in remote top floor offices behind many layers of security.

When Christine joined Victoria Police, she told a deputy she wanted to go out and talk to some of the thousands of employees scattered throughout Victoria. 'Why do you want to do that for? They'll only whinge!' was the response. Indeed they did complain. But it was the start of many people in the organisation, and outside it, feeling as though they could tell Christine important things and that they could trust her to listen and find ways to follow up.

Among the issues that were raised and she could act upon were physical conditions, such as more comfortable uniforms for the diversity of recruits that the Victoria Police was now targeting. Other actions included removing physical obstacles, such as 'the wall', a 6-foot high hurdle that potential recruits had to surmount to join the police. Women routinely failed this test. It was a historical criterion for selection, and not one that was relevant to contemporary police activities.

Throughout her time in office she identified herself as a woman, bringing her values as a woman to policing, in order to underline the importance of Victoria Police reflecting the diversity of the community it was serving. For example, and controversially at the time, Christine joined police in the gay pride march. Her experiences provide many examples of the importance of physical presence in testing and tragic circumstances. These included standing before the Police Armed Offenders and Drug squads and advising that they were going to be shut down; and at many blackened locations in rural Victoria after the 2009 bushfires, with people who had lost everything, including family members.

Leadership scholar Joanne Ciulla has also documented the importance of political leaders 'being there' in crisis situations. She contrasts the delayed arrival of President George Bush after Hurricane Katrina with the immediate presence of Bill Clinton at various national crises and emergencies during his presidency. 'Being there' conveys moral solidarity, commitment and concern. Presence is important symbolically as well as what leaders can then do.[4] Actual bodily presence can also empower and mobilise. In crisis situations, as I described in Chapter 9 'Being mindful in crises', a common reaction is for followers to abdicate responsibility and develop dependency on authority. Recovering and helping locals return to some kind of normality often requires leaders not to take all the work on but to respectfully give it back to affected groups and communities, then support, resource and empower them to assume responsibility.

LOOKING AFTER OTHER BODIES IN LEADERSHIP

People, their well-being and their flourishing, matter. Looking after the people who are part of one's organisation or sphere of influence is probably the most basic responsibility of leadership. Being open to this responsibility doesn't always mean protecting. In fact, it is often about challenging and supporting others to take calculated risks, to do things they may find difficult. Indigenous leader and school principal Chris Sarra got into trouble for his sometimes physical ways of tackling a distinctly physical problem.[5] Or more accurately, a key problem was the absence of physical bodies at school, a chronically high rate of student absenteeism. Chris set about shifting the school culture to one that valued physical presence and well-being. He rewarded attendance by taking the winners to lunch; he developed a motto and guiding philosophy for kids to be 'strong and smart'; he set about improving the school grounds to make it a good place for kids to hang out after hours because home was not always welcoming. He also used his own physicality, as a respected rugby player, to inspire the kids towards self-respect and achievement.

Another person whose leadership has been character-ised by care of bodies is Dale Fisher, now CEO of the Peter MacCallum Cancer Hospital in Melbourne. 'Petermac', as it is known, is one of Australia's oldest, most pre-eminent and deeply loved hospitals because of its positive impact on many thousands of cancer sufferers and their families. I first met Dale through Rhonda Galbally, who was at that time Chair of the Royal Women's Hospital in Melbourne. Rhonda was herself an unconventional pioneer in public health and health promo-tion: the first CEO of VicHealth, and inaugural founder of the OurCommunity organisation. Dale was appointed CEO of the Royal Women's Hospital in 2004, a position she held until 2013. Throughout that period, she systematically set about moving the Women's Hospital (literally as well as metaphorically, and drop-ping the 'Royal' from its title), from a traditional, hierarchical, male-dominated medical environment into being a highly customer-focused, leading-edge provider of women's health, at the front of worldwide research and initiatives to empower a diverse, multicultural patient base of women to look after their health and well-being.

Dale's approach to leadership has been radically different to her predecessors and other hospital CEOs. A former nurse brought up in country Victoria, she was and continues to be unafraid to be who she is and to bring her values, instincts and flair to the role. She has also been a fearless advocate for women and their health, through extraordinary growth in services and changes in the diversity of services and community groups served. Prior to her arrival, the Women's Hospital had been aligned with the Royal Children's Hospital. Mothers and babies were deemed to be a 'natural' pairing. But this pairing limited what the Women's Hospital could do and what it was to be about going forward. Dale has consistently been unafraid to take a gender perspective on medicine, arguing persuasively that medical and hospital care has suffered through, for example, medical research which draws on samples comprised substantially of men and then simply assumes that women will respond similarly.

A particular achievement in leading change while looking after bodies was moving the Women's Hospital from its old site where it had stood for 150 years down the road to new purpose-built premises. It was a highly emotional and symbolic move as other women's hospitals had been lost or swallowed up in big hospital mergers. Most staff initially did not want to move. Loyalties to, and camaraderie for, the old site was strong. There were stories and memories to be upheld. Many people had worked for the hospital for 30 years or more. Hundreds of thousands of babies had been born there.

Dale's achievement was to navigate a path which acknowledged the past with all its achievements and attachments but also engendered optimism and confidence in what the new facility represented for looking after women. Ultimately, the move went without a hitch. Over one day, every patient, baby and piece of equipment was moved from the old hospital down the road to the new. It was a journey where physicality mattered at many levels: the care for palpable, fragile bodies, the faith in the physical caring of staff and technologies, honouring the physical symbolism of the old place and memory anchored in bodies and new lives, and creating new physical spaces, images and symbols that would speak to the community about women in the new century.

WHY LEADERS NEED TO CARE ABOUT
THEIR OWN BODIES

In my experience, many people working in leadership 'get' that leadership is physical. They experience the negative physical effects of working long hours, of unrelenting pressure and the physical toll of stress and absences on themselves and their families. On the other hand, most recognise that the effective and inspiring leaders around them are those who are present, perceived as being physically grounded and genuine, not just because of what they say but because of how they are in the space between themselves and others. Leaders know that the important conversations they have are those where what's really going on is discussed, where employees, customers and other stakeholders feel heard and held by those running organisations.

Looking after oneself, and being caring and thoughtful about the physical well-being of those with whom one works, is valuable in and of itself. Of course, this must not be intrusive or experienced as unwanted solicitousness. Yet people who work in physically demanding occupations, such as police and correctional officers, are often working in cultures that are punishing and abusive. It is valuable to help them find ways of delivering leadership and what they need to do physically without mirroring punishing or self-punishing norms. In this view, good leadership is not about physically disciplining ourselves to get through the work. Rather, it is about shifting the emphasis in doing the work to enable others to be both effective and to look after themselves. I am not underestimating the difficulty of modelling supportive leadership in a culture which is punishing or neglectful. But what I have learned, and I hope has emerged from the examples in this chapter and throughout the book, is that sometimes physical gestures, acts of nurturance and care towards self and others, may be both radical and substantial in their positive impacts.

Throughout the last decade I have sometimes taught yoga alongside my leadership teaching. This has been in business school and executive education settings, as well as at my local yoga studio.[6] I have sometimes come away from classes feeling that I did far more good in that 60 minutes of breathing, stretching and relaxing than in a whole term of leadership classes. In the four-day Mindful Leadership program that Richard Searle and I have offered, I lead a daily yoga class. For many participants, it is the first time they have ever encountered yoga. Some have physical constraints (for example, have had knee or hip surgery), others feel physically embarrassed and awkward. They often feel, and say, they 'can't do' yoga! Yet when we work together gently stretching and feeling our breath and bodies, participants almost always experience the connection to their physicality positively. For example, for some it is as simple as remembering and re-experiencing their capacities to let go and relax. Individuals often rediscover focus, perspective and compassion for themselves through yoga practice. They will leave a session or class feeling more settled, able to accept and embrace whatever life is presenting them. Routinely on the Mindful Leadership program, yoga is one of the features of the program that participants value most and which they vow to continue in some form or another.

Emerging neuroscientific data supports that physical activities such as yoga changes brain structures with associated improvements in emotional state and executive and cognitive functions. For example, a pilot study showed participants in a yoga program later registered less anxiety and depression. Subsequent studies reported improved brain functioning in older adults as a result of an eight-week yoga course. Working memory capacity and task switching both improved, which are two common measures of executive function. The research that doctor and author Norman Doidge explores in his two books, *The Brain that Changes Itself* and *The Brain's Way of Healing*,

provide further evidence and case studies of the complex interactions between mind and body. Simple physical activities, such
as walking and systematically exercising targeted muscles, restore
and enhance brain activity and broader functioning.

Our bodies and physicality in leadership are gateways to
important forms of intelligence, to wisdom and mindfulness. They provide us with ways of noticing and revaluing the
present, of experiencing the full richness of the people and situations around us. Physicality is not something to be ignored,
suppressed or overcome in leadership, but a means of helping us
live and lead more fully.

Thirteen

TUNING INTO THE SENSES

We are built to take delight in our world with our senses
of sight, smell and touch.
Joanna Macy

I am lucky enough to live in a part of suburban Melbourne that opens the day with birdsong. In particular, a pair of magpies resides in the top branches of our neighbours' very tall Norfolk Island pine tree. I've called the magpies Carol and Mike, after our neighbours. Each morning around the time I am waking, or sometimes when I'm meditating, or emptying the dishwasher, they launch into their dazzling repertoire. Wherever my thoughts are at that moment—whether it is important, such as a troubling section of something I am writing, or more likely a reminder not to forget to put the rubbish out—I am brought into the moment. Like the Buddhist clocks that gong at preset intervals to bring us back to the present, Carol and Mike remind me to notice this particular morning.

As I write this . . . there they are . . . there they go again . . . and again . . . I have a choice. I can ignore or not hear them, which happens often enough. I can get involved in thinking about magpies and how they do it. I can note that Australian, as opposed to English, magpies are widely loved for their amazing songs (and occasionally loathed for their territorial behaviour). I can remember that each call is distinctive, learned and passed down largely by father magpie. Their repertoires are rated as among the world's most complex and dazzling birdsong. I can then Google and research magpie song . . . Or I can be more in the moment and listen harder, clinging to capture the notes, to see if each call has the same melody or whether there is improvisation, to my ear anyway, this morning.

But these understandings, rich and interesting as they are, are not the real gift here. The gift is the truly amazing call to notice what is here and alongside us now. These reminders to be present that come through our senses can't be planned or summoned up according to when it suits us: 'I'll just listen later.' They are here and can be given attention. With this they remind us that we are here, in this moment, in our lives. There is a purity and simplicity to these moments that must be valued: extraordinary, yet available for us in the mundane and ordinary.

HOW IS BEING SENSUAL A PATH TO MINDFULNESS?

There is a common misunderstanding that to become mindful, one must reject the senses. One must resolutely turn away from the tempting outer world and focus on inward mind discipline. The assumption here—underpinned by various religious and enlightenment philosophies—is that the mind is the trusted source of wisdom, while the senses divert and distract us.

In fact, despite the importance Buddhism gives to the mind, most teachers suggest that the senses, such as listening to sounds, are very reliable ways in to mindfulness, not disruptive of it. For example, highly respected mindfulness researcher and teacher Jon Kabat-Zinn devotes a substantial part of his lovely book

Coming to Our Senses to having us re-experience and revalue the senses as a gateway to mindfulness, to living life with full presence.

Certainly, if you find yourself captured in thoughts, somewhere else altogether in your mind, allowing yourself to feel the air on your skin, savouring the *crema* on coffee or the taste of lunch is a simple way to come back to the present. Far from distracting us, being attuned to the senses can enable us to be fully here. A not uncommon exercise in helping people experience mindfulness is inviting them to eat an orange, a raisin, or even a chocolate, slowly. Try it now, or soon. If you have a cup of coffee or tea on your desk or close by, pause and turn away from your book, your computer or phone. Take your time and give your whole self to being curious about the sensations of savouring or drinking. If you get caught up in judging or evaluating—this coffee isn't as hot as I'd like it, that café must have changed the milk they are using—notice and return your attention to the sensations, the feel in the mouth, the visual or aromatic feast that many simple foods offer.

By taking time and noticing the particular stages of sensation, of touch, smell, sound and taste, of crunch, chew or squish, of juice and saliva, we are brought back to the moment. Instead of wolfing down food, this process encourages a gratitude and appreciation for aesthetic objects and pleasurable experiences that we usually take for granted or don't even notice. In a larger ontological way, giving attention to senses can create a changed experience of time. As described by Kabat-Zinn, 'Mindfulness can restore our moments to us by reminding us that it is possible and even valuable to linger with them, dwell in them, feel them through all our senses and know them in awareness.'[1]

SENSUALITY AND LEADERSHIP

'Well,' you might be saying, 'that's all very lovely for enjoying oranges but what have the senses and paying attention to them got to do with leadership?' The words 'sensible' and 'sensual' come from the same Latin root—*sensibilis*—which is to do with the senses. Being 'sensible' 'sensitive' and showing 'good' or 'common' sense have long been recognised as virtues in interactions with others, so it is interesting to speculate on how and why sensuality has been given such different meaning.[2] Yet I want to suggest several reasons why the senses, and opening oneself to being sensual, is valuable in leadership. The first is that the senses potentially give us a lot of data about what's going on and what matters in organisations, workplaces, with ourselves and with each other. It is information which we sometimes ignore with regrettable consequences. In an unusual workplace study, researchers Kathleen Riach and Samantha Warren explored the powerful role of smell—for example, how people smelled to each other and the effect of lingering lunch smells—in underpinning people's attitudes to work.[3] They show how central the senses, and particularly smell, is as part of the 'ephemeral affective "glue" that floats between and around working bodies', playing an active role in constituting relationships and potentially enhancing the richness, diversity and pleasure of daily work life, or conversely literally souring people's experiences.[4]

Increasingly, researchers have been turning to the arts and similar contexts which involve improvisation and creativity with groups *in the moment* to explore the importance of the physical, sensual and aesthetic in accomplishing leadership. For example, in an orchestra, to produce a beautiful or aesthetically pleasing outcome, the role of leader/conductor is pivotally about the senses.[5] It can include the following:

- sensing the movement and pace of an ensemble's learning
- modelling for the group how to act and move with feeling
- with the conductor's own senses and physicality, through posture and movement, disrupting habituated or stale responses by musicians and choristers
- encouraging the release of physical energy and agency
- creating a collective rhythmic intensity and tone that, in turn, is experienced by the audience aesthetically and emotionally.

Conductors have been known to dramatically slow down their arm movements, reduce the size of physical actions to barely perceptible or even lie on the floor in order to provoke a more sense-driven, less technical or habituated response from their musicians.

But it's not just conductors, theatre or dance directors who need to be concerned with the senses. Leadership roles across sectors often require leaders to be able to *sense* a team's response to key events or movement towards values and goals. These shifts are sometimes more able to be registered through the senses than concretised in numbers of clients or earnings.

As the physical and embodied dimensions of leadership have increasingly been explored in research, the sensibilities of the leader become a focus of interest. In my own research I have observed particularly non-traditional leaders grapple with the unacknowledged dynamics of what kind of body a leader should inhabit, yet trusting their senses to guide them in creating more empowering conditions for the people they are leading. While such practices are observable and palpable (for example, in the work of many arts and Indigenous leaders), other more mainstream leaders such as hospital CEO Dale Fisher, featured in the preceding chapter, do not ignore their gut, senses and their instincts, especially when seeking to influence groups, such as senior clinicians, to innovate.

At a personal level, being attuned to the senses can assist in leadership. We can often sense in our body, in the prickling of skin or sudden shift in attentive silence, that something important has just happened. In a meeting, someone may have made an unusual observation or spoken with surprising intensity; a junior member of the group may have been summarily silenced; or a group may find itself in a place of lightness and appreciation of each other. In such cases we sense before our mind has begun to 'make' sense. Tuning into these momentary sensations, prompting ourselves to give deeper attention, can thus allow hunches to be assessed and potentially acted upon.

A second reason why sense data is valuable for leaders is connected with emotions. As I explore in Chapter 16 'Feeling', workplaces generally encourage employees to suppress their feelings. In management theory, the good organisation is one in which emotions are either absent or are tightly managed around a template of prescribed positive emotion. Thus, the young McDonalds employee is schooled in being bubbly and cheerful, the consultant in being confident, trust-inducing and upbeat. At a more senior level, I often work with leaders who have been advised that they need to be 'less emotional'. This advice is particularly given to women, and it is sometimes a mechanism by which organisations project onto individuals feelings which may be widely shared but are disowned. Because many workplaces are, in fact, rife with feelings, at all levels of intensity, tuning into the senses is a good way of being open to hearing—and responding to—one's own and others' emotions before they erupt or become hardened into bitterness or cynicism.[6]

For individual leaders, giving attention to senses, and then the sense responses from the feelings and emotions which sometimes follow in their wake, can be particularly useful in coping with difficult or stressful circumstances. A common example is public speaking. For some leaders, a high-pressure presentation or speaking publicly is preceded by a churning stomach, dryness in the mouth, shortness of breath, a flushed face or nausea. Each of these sense experiences can speedily tip over into overwhelming feelings of imminent failure or shame, of being an imposter or inadequate to the task. If we can, in the moment, notice these sensory responses, we can often then pause and avoid launching into habitual rushes of bad feelings, or 'stories' about ourselves like 'I'm hopeless at this' or 'These things always end in disaster for me'.[7] Because sensations are immediate, they can often be responded to by, for example, some deep breathing or drinking a glass of water. Providing some momentary mindfulness, a sensory response thus enables us to pause and then make a choice about whether certain feelings inevitably follow.

Creativity is a third reason why leaders might want to give attention to senses. Sense data and developing forms of intelligence oriented around the senses are key to our capacity to think laterally across categories, to relinquish self-judgement, to adopt a permissive or experimental approach in learning something new or being resilient after failure.

One of the pieces of assessment I sometimes ask MBA students to undertake is to read a biography of a leader. I encourage them to look widely across all fields of endeavour to select leaders including scientists, novelists, artists and activists. I refuse to make recommendations but I strongly discourage them from the usual suspects: politicians, sportspeople, business and corporate types such as Richard Branson (though I was unsuccessful in dissuading one student to choose the now-disgraced cyclist Lance Armstrong who was then at the height of success!). I use this form of assessment for several reasons. First, it sometimes encourages (dare I say 'forces') them to see leadership in its broader and more interesting forms. Second, good biographies provide a different way of writing about a leader's experiences that give a more sensory, physical and non-cognitively mediated account of a life, and motivation, in leadership. The beauty of the environment, the puzzle of a natural phenomena, the gut impact of a social issue or a personal dilemma can be grasped. For the students, reading these stories can sometimes open their own more nuanced sensory appreciation, enabling them to see the phenomena of leadership with a freshness and liveliness that is so often absent from textbooks.

Finally, and perhaps most importantly, the senses are valuable not because of what they help us to know or do but as part of living. They are valuable for themselves. The production of leadership has usually been framed as a rational rather than sensual activity. But sensuality is not separate from good leadership, it is integral to it. It is through the senses that we come alive and feel pleasure in being in the moment. As I explore in the next chapter, pleasure is often registered through the tactile—a child reaching up to hold our hand, or the thrilling lift in the chest as a beautiful voice soars. Tuning into the senses offers one pathway to experiencing pleasure in leadership work.

Fourteen

FINDING PLEASURE

Life must be studied, relished, meditated upon.
I dwell on any pleasure that comes to me.
I do not skim over it, but plumb its depths.
Michel de Montaigne

Pleasure is rarely mentioned in connection with leadership. Yet re-finding and recognising the pleasure in our leadership work provides an antidote to the denial of embodied, sensual know-ledge that is so pervasive in leadership theory. Being open to pleasure—defined broadly—enables good leadership to thrive and organisations to nourish their occupants.

In this chapter I explore meanings of pleasure in leadership, including the route by which I have come to find pleasure and a sense of renewal in my own work. I provide some examples from others to show how pleasure may be a powerful part of what both nourishes the leader and is impactful and helpful for the people they are working with. What constitutes pleasure for you? What comes to mind for you may be a different mixture to what I describe here, but my hope is that the ideas and exam-ples in this chapter may cause you to pause, notice, and perhaps rediscover and relish the diverse pleasures in your work.

PLEASURE IN LEADERSHIP

Ideas and words like pleasure cannot be understood outside of the social and cultural contexts that produce them. Hence the idea of pleasure is often seen narrowly as a simple, hedonistic seeking of gratification—as perhaps the opposite of the sober, responsibility-embracing work of leadership.

But I want to suggest that this is a construction that doesn't necessarily help leaders or leadership. The notion of pleasure-seeking as greedy or selfish, as to do with base bodily hungers, is just another form of the dichotomising of mind and body that I've critiqued elsewhere in my research and this book. It's another unhelpful habit of dividing and privileging some experience over others—there is work and there is pleasure, just as there is mind and there is body. We should question these mentally-mediated divisions.

Pleasure, I'll suggest, can encompass many things: moments, interactions, relationships, experiences, perceptions, observations, body sensations. Pleasure is related to happiness, but is more fleeting, more moment-to-moment and deserves to be given attention in its own right in our lives. An experience of pleasure can be very simple: delighting in someone dressed eccentrically or outrageously on a train; reading a moving story; noticing the grace and dignity of a person you are lucky enough to encounter. Pleasure is also the taste of a cold beer on a hot day, or one of my four-year-old grandchildren describing dinosaurs, slowly but triumphantly, as 'extinct'!

MY JOURNEY IN FINDING PLEASURE

My own journey in exploring the place of pleasure in leadership began many years ago as part of rethinking leadership and my own purpose and intent in the work I do (see also Chapter 18

'Clarifying purpose, going for happiness'). I argued in *Leadership for the Disillusioned* that leadership should be about supporting freedom, and not, as I was often observing, about enslaving people in work that was unsustainable and made them miserable. For my own part, and due to several of the circumstances I have already described, I started to notice that life was short! It was important not to suffer too much and not to put off enjoying oneself until next month or next year. That moment might not come. So how was I to find a different way of working and providing a role model that did not sacrifice life to work, that found delight and pleasure in the day-to-day, not just on holidays?

What I then embarked on, in fits and starts, might be characterised by some as a spiritual journey. But I am wary of that word 'spiritual'. It has a lot of baggage associated with its use to do with being above the body and not 'in' the world. In contrast, my pursuit of meaning, purpose and pleasure has been anchored in the whole 'blooming, buzzing confusion' of the lived world— to borrow the famous phrase from American philosopher William James.

As I began exploring these ideas, I found that many writers, particularly women, had already begun reclaiming notions of eros and love, desire and pleasure as valuable aspects of experience; these had been written out of many 'serious' accounts of philosophy, education, theories of being and knowing (ontologies and epistemologies). While conservative norms are that knowledge-building is an often solitary and arm's-length mental exchange, writers such as educationalist bell hooks argue against perpetuating the gendered and racist institutionalised 'manners' of the academy. In her view, eroticism and passion are often classroom sparks for transgression and a truly democratic education.[1] Similarly, in the context of teaching, education academic Erica McWilliam maintains, 'If teaching-as-usual is unpleasant, dull and restrictive, then "good", exciting, motivating teaching is erotic, passionate, dangerous, and evokes body pleasure.' Being happy and satisfied as teachers and learners is at least as important in education as acquiring knowledge, perhaps more so.[2] While these writers are talking about educational contexts, their arguments have relevance for many leadership situations, too, where empowering others and generating new understandings *are* the work.

Instead of pursuing a love of wisdom—the traditional preoccupation of universities—philosopher Luce Irigaray advises us to pursue the wisdom of love. Here, heart and mind, body and breath are united in the search to live better with oneself and with others in the world.[3] From a very different perspective, educationalist Julie Laible suggests we put love at the heart of doing research. In a 'loving epistemology', knowledge-building and theory-making must make sense to, and be useful and empowering for, those we research.[4]

I have drawn on these radically different views about what good leadership might involve in my research with various colleagues. For example, with medical researcher Mary Black, at a time when both of us were combining our role as professors with caring for young babies, we gave a conference presentation and paper entitled 'Breasts, babies and universities: Reflections of two lactating professors'. The paper attempted to show how academic leadership cultures were inimical to the grounded, embodied but very worthwhile activity of caring for babies and we tried to get the paper published. The response was that it was 'whingeing'.

Much of the research on women in leadership is met with a similarly dismissive but perhaps more polite response. It shows that women continue to experience substantial obstacles in aspiring to leadership, obstacles which are not to do with their performance or effectiveness but about how they are judged as unsuitable for leadership, because they are women, with women's bodies and physicality. The same research often implies that the only possible response women leaders can adopt is camouflage, denial or suppression of their sensual and sexual selves.

In another piece of research which also focused initially on academic leadership, Emma Bell and I felt like it was time to ask how the pleasure and eros had been removed from life as an academic and how these aspects might be reclaimed.[5] The word eroticism derives from eros, meaning *love*, which includes imaginative love, the prospect of love and a love of wisdom as well as sexual passion. While eroticism might be a feeling between people, a sense of anticipation, implied attraction or pleasure, it is related first and foremost to love, rather than sex or calculations of sexual appeal. In our view, eros defined as sensuality, connection and love has, and should have, a place in academic life. The thrill of great teaching; the closeness and nurturance often involved in research supervision and collaborations; the delight in going after bold new ideas with colleagues or discovering fresh evidence for important phenomena—there is a lot of pleasure in academic life which potentially conveys itself positively and makes a big difference to students and educational outcomes, as well as teachers and researchers.

In our writing together, Emma and I have sought to reinstate into explorations of women's leadership evidence that eros and opportunities to pursue pleasure are not just present in the work but legitimate things to look for. Although initially focused on academia, our subsequent research extends to leadership more broadly. It is inappropriate to pretend that sexuality and eroticism aren't often part of the leadership process. When I think about my own classrooms and the leadership of myself and others in them, particularly those which are intense or extended or both, there is attraction, spark, passion, energy and eros.

I'm thinking of a spontaneous dance that happened between two rather buttoned-up members of my last part-time MBA class that, of course, drew rounds of applause and whistles from the class.

Psychiatrist and Buddhist Mark Epstein also argues that notions of pleasure and desire have been recast in unhelpful ways by religion and other ideologies such as consumerism and critiques of them. His view, in his book *Open to Desire,* is that desire can be an ally in intimacy, and in creating a deep connection in the space between self and other.[6] In this frame, desire is more than a craving for what culture has conditioned us to want. We can learn how to desire differently, instead of being exploited or manipulated by it.

All relations, including in work and leadership, can be driven by objectification. We feel desire or 'in need' of something from another, whether it be approval, a promotion or acceptance, and often condemn other people to the role of simply gratifying desires. Yet Epstein argues it is in mature understanding of this desire, rather than being captive of it, that important emotional and spiritual work takes place. The paradox, as expressed by Epstein, is 'how much we need each other to make freedom possible'.[7]

PLEASURE IN LEADERSHIP WORK

Tracy Castelino is a consultant offering services to case workers and organisations—including charitable, health and training organisations, women's agencies aimed at domestic violence, counselling services and local councils—involved in work such as domestic violence education, cross-cultural awareness and challenging sexism. We have been working together for several years, after she came to me initially for some help in considering her career options: Should she build on her PhD and pursue an academic path? Seek a role in an existing social welfare organisation? Or try to build a business practice doing the work she is passionate about—supporting women who are victims of domestic violence and changing systems to better empower and resource women.

Combating domestic violence and supporting workers in the sector is a tough area. Workers are routinely dealing with traumatised victims and survivors, dangerous perpetrators and insufficient resources. The pain and trauma of frontline workers routinely folds back into other layers of organisations, with managers and leaders up the line experiencing the stress and strain. In Australia, after long-term political and institutional denial of the scale and seriousness of the problem—more women die from domestic violence than any major illness, such as cancer or heart disease—resources have belatedly flowed into the system in the last few years. Yet many workers—with their own experiences to draw on—believe the wrong things are being supported. Work with men and perpetrators is needed, but some maintain this area is being over-resourced, again placing women and their urgent needs at the bottom of the pile.

Tracy is a highly skilled and caring person whose journey, as she has developed her work and built a profile as a respected and courageous consultant to the sector, has been wonderful to watch. There are many strengths I could describe about the way she has gone about her own leadership in the sector. But I want to focus here on how she has increasingly found herself gaining pleasure and satisfaction from her consulting and support activities, especially her work advising leaders and managers in local government and other agencies seeking to have impact on the epidemic of violence against women and girls. This involves, as she says, 'taking care of the space', but also challenging groups often dominated by white men to own their privilege, to keep women and structural gender issues front and centre, to argue powerfully and movingly for change.

A petite woman of Indian heritage, Tracy comes to her role equipped with a fierce intelligence and passionate convictions. Her own history and some of the victimisation and marginalisation she and her family have suffered sometimes meant that when times got tough, as they inevitably do in such difficult work, a lot of self-judgement followed. Rage and anger were understandable and familiar places when faced with yet another instance of women not being heard, or resources being misused.

We have done quite a lot of work together on mindfulness, a concept that she was already familiar with through her partner and other connections. What Tracy started doing, partially as a result of that work, was pausing in the middle of the workshops she runs, noticing what was unfolding, being moved by the work that she and participants were doing, expressing that and feeling joy and satisfaction from it.

When I showed Tracy a draft of this chapter to ensure she was comfortable with what I had written, she was keen for me to also describe 'how you have worked with me, supported me to understand and practice embodiment in the work . . . as for me this has allowed me to breathe in the pleasure, the connecting points, the learning moments and engaging with people differently'. This embodied and mindful way of working has involved Tracy trusting herself to go 'off script', to notice the engagement and the experiences of participants and herself in the moment. These aspects of mindful embodied practice—the noticing and then embodying the experiences—have allowed, in her words, 'feelings of joy, appreciation, concern or pain' to be expressed by participants in the group work and a 'purposeful and emotionally tangible care' to be created.

I wanted to use Tracy's leadership as an example because it seems a quite astounding achievement. In such a difficult area of work where people are often feeling embattled, the mixture of her experience, knowledge and expertise with embodied mindfulness creates an environment of support and learning, but also often beauty, pleasure and hope for participants and for herself.

Fifteen

OPENING TO CREATIVITY

Each of us literally chooses, by his way of attending to things, what sort of universe he shall appear to inhabit.
William James

In *My Stroke of Insight,* Jill Bolte Taylor, herself a neuroanatomist, describes in gripping detail how her mind changed during and after suffering a stroke at age 37.[1] Her moving, first-hand experience describes how, with the disabling of the speech and 'self-talk' parts of the brain, she was no longer so invested in herself or so tied up in notions of how she should be.[2] Freed of internalised prescriptions about who she was and what she should do, greater openness, permissiveness and creativity followed.

My own experience preparing to write this book is a much less dramatic, but still close to home, encounter with how the conscious mind can crush creativity, and then stop action dead in its tracks. For several years leading up to 2015, I said to myself things like, 'The world doesn't need another leadership book', 'The books I have already written say what I believe and want to share', 'There are other good books out there on mindfulness', 'No-one will want to read what I have to say about leading mindfully'. All of the above may be true, but the turning point was giving myself permission and setting an intention. I carved out six months from my diary and only accepted enough work to pay the school fees. I started—scarily—telling people I was writing a book about mindfulness and leadership. I waited for them to express the doubts and cynicism that my conscious mind had long rehearsed. When they didn't, I started to enjoy myself. While I was writing it, more internal voices appeared: 'Heavy-hitting leaders won't read this', 'It's not serious research', 'Your academic colleagues will scoff', 'With so much personal experience included, the book will be dismissed as sentimental and confessional', and so on. But a further reminder from mindfulness came that these are just thoughts, just the way the thinking mind works, and not to pay too much heed to them. This recognition about the mind continues to be deeply helpful to me, especially when contemplating risky or radical opportunities.

Research shows that to allow ourselves to initially be creative, and then act on that creativity, we must find ways of turning down parts of our habitual ways of thinking, especially the judging and self-judging parts associated with language. In the field of jazz improvisation, surgeon and musician Charles Limb pioneered specially designed neuroimaging techniques to capture what happened neurologically to jazz musicians as they improvised. His research revealed that frontal lobe parts of the brain that are involved in aspects of consciousness, such as self-monitoring and memory, are effectively *turned off* during improvisation to allow other aspects, such as those parts involved in visual and motor coordination, to be switched on.

Further evidence from both neuroscience and arts leadership tells us that the part of our brain that we rely on for our usual thinking can be a tyrant. It takes over, assumes space and importance, and can shut us down. It issues orders and judges us. It behaves in such a self-important fashion that we start to treat it as the God-like arbiter of the truth—a truth or reality that must be listened to. Buddhist writer Tenzin Palmo describes it as the 'difficult to please' travelling companion in our lives, the one who 'endlessly complains and tells you how useless you are'.[3] She suggests that while the mind is our life companion, it doesn't have to be this one, telling us this story.

What has all this got to do with leadership? Not all of leadership work requires creativity, but most leadership benefits from aspects of being creative that are also, as I've suggested in this book, part of what mindfulness offers. The practices of creativity I discuss here include:

- intentionality, setting a desire or purpose to be open
- trusting the senses and what they can tell you
- patience and valuing time
- stillness and silence
- self-authorisation towards freedom and permissiveness.

Creativity, I suggest, requires in some measure each of the above, which mindfulness also supports. But leadership, as I hope to show in this chapter, can benefit from them, too. While Bolte Taylor had the unwelcome intervention of a stroke to help her find creativity, artists and artistic leaders know a lot about how to 'turn down' certain parts of their minds to allow other parts to flourish. Increasing research demonstrates the value of these processes to leadership more generally, not just in the areas of the arts but in all those areas of leadership that require courage or boldness, when the support of others is not present, or when intuition or gut feel is what we're going on.[4]

OPENING TO CREATIVITY IN LEADERSHIP— LEARNING FROM ARTISTIC LEADERS

Film-maker and artist David Lynch has spoken movingly about his understanding of several elements of being creative.[5] First, in terms of getting ideas, he says, there is something very powerful about setting an intention or desire. Using the analogy of fishing, he says that desire for an idea is like the bait on a hook. You put the bait in the water and you wait, patiently. A fish will come, you reel it up. You don't know what it will be, maybe just a fragment. You feel it, see it, smell it. Perhaps it becomes bigger bait as you throw it back in and see what it attracts.

Second, stillness and silence are key companions in this process. Like some music composers, Lynch suggests that silence is often more powerful than noise. Supporting the creative process is a beautiful, infinite silence within us all, one he says holds the answers to the mysteries we are seeking to understand.

Lynch makes the point that we don't know what is 'an idea' until it enters the conscious mind. The subtle and sensual processes of giving time and patience, then openness and curiosity, then more time to feel and smell, to perhaps put it back in and see what the fragment attracts, are all processes that occur before much involvement of the conscious mind. It requires different things to cognitive working, including recognition of the potential beauty in the fragment. It is important to nurture it, to give attention to it, perhaps by writing the idea down at this stage, but in a way which captures its vividness.

Then there is the process of working on the idea. Is it a collaborative or solo activity? This is a question that many artists are asked. How do you ensure artistic outcomes reflect collaborative or community processes of production or ownership, while not sacrificing individual vision? For Lynch and some other artistic leaders with whom I have worked, these are not useful questions. What is more important is getting 'in there', working and endlessly talking to people, 'acting' and then 'reacting'. Lynch observes, 'It is so much fun to get in there, to get *filthy*. There's *so much joy in there*.'

Lynch insists he is not trying to answer the big questions or tell us how to live with his art. He is not trying to tell anybody anything. It is more a matter of getting out of the chair, inviting experiment, and exploring through the senses the mysteries of life.

BEING BOLD

The question of how leaders can be bold and what gets in the way of being creative and bold is a question my colleague and friend Christine Nixon and I have been pondering and asking audiences with whom we work. Boldness seems to be in short supply in organisations, and yet often important challenges require leaders to think outside the square, to trust their intuition and to share it with influential others, to turn off the judging voice that says 'That won't work'. Christine has explored some of the institutional and contextual reasons that stop public sector leaders being bold. But when we ask audiences what gets in the way, people often volunteer that it is fear and worry about the risks of failure and looking stupid that stops them backing themselves, speaking out or trying to do things differently.

In terms of being bold in leadership, Director of the Bendigo Art Gallery Karen Quinlan comes immediately to mind. The world of Australian visual arts leadership—large gallery management—has historically been elitist and masculine. Although in more experimental areas of the arts, all kinds of innovative approaches to leadership flourish, the leadership of galleries has typically been seen as the domain of credible male art historians who have steadily built, from curatorial roles, artistic reputation and respect to lead.

Though Quinlan was a teacher and curator, she does not easily fit this model. Since taking up the position of director in 2000, she has executed an extraordinarily bold and different vision for the Bendigo Art Gallery. By any economic and cultural measure she has been a star, garnering previously unheard of national and international audiences for exhibitions.[6] Unassuming as she is, Karen has been at the helm of a wave of rethinking regional art galleries, to the extent that others seek to 'do a Bendigo' and emulate 'the Quinlan effect'.

Bendigo has staged hugely successful exhibitions which depart from traditional conceptions of high art—often masculine, conservative and painterly in their focus. These exhibitions include 'The Golden Age of Couture: Paris and London 1947–57' (2009), 'The White Wedding Dress: 200 Years of Wedding Fashion' (2011), 'Grace Kelly: Style Icon' (2012), 'The Body Beautiful in Ancient Greece' and 'Undressed: 350 Years of Underwear Fashion' (2014). Lest one be tempted to think Quinlan is only interested in bodies and clothing, there was also the highly prestigious 'Genius and Ambition: Royal Academy of Arts' exhibition, also in 2014. Alongside some of these 'blockbusters' have been arguably even more innovative exhibitions of photography, sculpture, visual and textile art. In each case Quinlan recognised that there was a powerful artistic story to be told, one that hadn't been told, and that audiences would come to view. The subjects are diverse: Australian women photographers, Victorian traditions of 'Looking for Faeries', dolls and Hollywood, but they are subjects that are often outside the usual gallery 'canon'. Quinlan has a background as a teacher and curator in textiles, but these initiatives do more than play to her interests. They stretch notions of what art is about, and they put the body, style, sexuality and gender into the gallery space in provocative and educational ways.

Quinlan has clearly been creative in these initiatives but she is also exercising leadership. Her risks have been calculated ones. She knew that a large part—perhaps as much as 80 to 90 per cent—of gallery audiences are women. She recognised there were areas of artistic endeavour that would appeal to this audience but had been neglected. She was right. She is also collaborative in her creativity. While some of the seeds of exhibitions have come from her, she insists that the success of the Bendigo Art Gallery and its cultural impact are due to a much wider group, including her boss, who has empowered and trusted her and has driven the bigger vision for Bendigo as a cultural and tourist centre; her team at the gallery who bring their curatorial, educational and other talents ('It's good for me not to be there sometimes, to give them space,' she says); and the wider Bendigo community, sponsors and supporters who have taken pride in and been part of the unique cultural identity created.

Where does the boldness, the capacity to see opportunity and willingness to take risks come from?

Quinlan is the fourth of five children and she developed early the appetite to pit herself towards a big challenge, to work hard and not expect things to come to her. She listens to lots of people and is a trusted friend and ally for many artists and custodians of collections. She is patient. Planting lots of seeds for future shows through her contacts and conversations, she positions herself as open and more than willing to exploit opportunities to tell powerful artistic stories—usually that others in her sector have not noticed or have dismissed. She puts herself in the way of things, notices details and trusts these instincts. After she saw a 'Ned Kelly' tattoo on a passing leg one day, she and her team asked themselves why Australian bushranger Ned Kelly continued to resonate so much in the public imagination. The Kelly story offered an opportunity for the gallery: the potential to bring original artefacts such as Ned's iconic armour to Bendigo for the first time, a collision of history and art which might draw in different audiences such as students of Australian history. In 2015, those seeds became the 'Imagining Ned' exhibition.

Quinlan is open, allowing good instincts and sensibilities—her own and others'—to surface. However, she is also a risk-taker, often not going with the crowd or her peers on artistic matters. She challenges, asks, and is not awed by the weight of international art wisdom. But what happens with her ego at these junctures? Has she been worried about being knocked back when she has rocked up to prestigious institutions in the art world, such as the Royal Academy, asking, 'Had you thought about coming to Australia?'

The answers to these questions offer further valuable lessons in creative leadership. Quinlan's approaches to prestigious institutions and collectors are backed by research and checked out with a firm grip on costs, audiences and what's possible. She doesn't go to the New York Metropolitan Museum of Art. But the Royal Academy is a group of artists who had never shown their collection before. The other part of the answer is more personal and it is that she doesn't have too much ego. She's had lots of knock-backs. She's asked many large Australian galleries whether she can borrow their artworks and got lots of 'nos'. It's part of the process, 'taking the good with the bad', allowing self and team to mend. She's learned to enjoy the job, surrounded herself with a hand-picked team, kept space for herself through her long runs. Dispensing with the hubris that often marks the style of her peers has created for Quinlan, and her team, an exciting platform for leadership.

PART THREE

LEADING WITH HEART

In this third and final part of *Leading Mindfully* I turn to explore the possibility of leading with heart. What does it mean to lead with an open heart?[1] There are several ideas I want to convey in this section of the book. The first is that to lead well, you need to do it with more than your head. As will be clear from the book so far, I believe that—in leadership theory certainly and probably in leadership practice, too—there has been an overemphasis on leadership as a project of the head, of thinking, cognitive complexity and sophistication as the things to be aiming for.

My MBA students certainly expect that they will be taught ways of thinking in my leadership class. Yet they remain ineffective if they stay in their head. When people treat others transactionally (however cleverly), offer little of themselves or remain unmoved by their colleagues, they generally fail to exercise any leadership. Leadership inevitably involves dealing with feelings and emotions, including your own, and effective leadership means a readiness to lead in the territory of difficult emotional issues, drawing on your own emotions.

In Buddhist philosophy, the mind and the heart are the same thing. The role of leadership within these teachings is building a strong, warm and compassionate heart. This is not a sentimental or indulgent activity. It's a life's work, requiring practice and perseverance, and it's where many other good qualities come from, including wisdom and, often, insight. Cultivating compassion—a feeling for others and a desire to help relieve their suffering—is thus a very practical activity in leadership. Increasing amounts of research indicate that there are demonstrated benefits to those being led and those doing the leading when it is undertaken with kindness and compassion.[2] These benefits include physiological impacts on health and well-being, reduced stress and experiencing a fresh sense of effectiveness and purpose.

To lead with heart also means to lead with courage, to stand up for what you believe in and place a belief in what matters at the centre of what you do. Exploring and being connected to one's purpose has many benefits in leadership. It equips us with criteria to decide how to act and where to spend one's energies. It also often helps to inspire others and makes those around leaders feel connected to worthwhile ends.

Having said all that, I don't want leading with heart to sound overly pious or grandiose. I'm not suggesting we must all be warriors or martyrs sacrificing ourselves and our enjoyment of life to grand causes. Quite the contrary. I believe that leading with heart involves cultivating an openness to life as it is now, to allowing ourselves to live according to what helps us be happy and fulfilled. Leading with heart is less about erecting grand plans and monuments and more about allowing natural instincts for connection and fulfilment to flourish.

Sixteen

FEELING

*Emotions are critical to everything a leader must do: build
trust, strengthen relationships, set a vision, focus energy,
get people moving, make trade-offs, make tough decisions
and learn from failure.*
Doug Sundheim

Leadership is a lonely, self-contained, consuming business and
expressing emotions and feelings is dangerous—or so common
understandings go. Similarly, conventional wisdom is that the
role of the leader is to be tough and stoic, that it is unhelpful to
others and can undermine the necessary confidence and resilience to do the job if one is vulnerable to emotion. It says that
love is for personal lives and that leaders are best to keep their
feelings of compassion and love at home. Many leaders and
aspiring leaders say to me that leadership takes over, that the
only way to do it is 24/7, completely focused.

Leaders keep their own feelings at bay and seek to curb
others' emotional expressions largely because it is safer that way.
They sometimes confuse leadership with being in control, or at
least looking like it, when in fact the opposite is more often true.
Almost always the things that get in the way of leadership being

enacted are unexpressed or repressed feelings. Allowing feelings in, and encouraging people to permit themselves to feel, is the gateway to inspiring and influencing others.

As a case study of the power of learning to work with feelings in leadership, I'd like to draw on some of the MBA and EMBA students with various kinds of medical training who I have worked with over many years. These include doctors, surgeons, psychiatrists, specialists of various kinds whose jobs increasingly involve leadership and for which their medical training has left them unprepared. Their jobs involve leading teams, mentoring juniors, representing their colleagues institutionally and professionally, advocating for innovation, research, more resources or better patient care, and so on. I want to draw on some of these individuals as case studies because in their work, they regularly deal with intense feelings, such as those of patients who have to be informed of difficult diagnoses and poor prognoses. Many have also had training in, or been exposed to, mentors and norms that dictate tight regulation and management of their own feelings in the highly skilled technical work they do.

When they arrive in a Leadership and Change MBA class, individuals with medical backgrounds and training often show particular strengths. They are highly intelligent, with a strong work ethic and a determination to do well. They also have an overriding commitment to patient welfare—to doing whatever their expertise allows to enable survival, in the first instance, and then recovery—primarily physical but also psychological. These part-time students are already under intense workload pressures and working very long hours. In being interested in management and leadership, they are already different from many of their medical colleagues who eschew management, choosing to pursue clinical work, at a distance from health leadership and wider public health issues.

My observation about these class participants is that their

very strengths in clinical and professional practice bring challenges for leadership. First, they often struggle with recognising and allowing expression of their own and others' emotions. In a class setting, their first impulse can often be a genuinely felt desire to protect and shield others from difficult circumstances. As a teacher whose role it is to sometimes 'turn up the heat' on a group in order to have them leave the certainty of what they know, I have found it is often the medically trained members of the group whose anxiety levels go up most quickly. The experience of exposing people to discomfort and anxiety frequently goes against everything they've learned. What happens? Individuals step in and use their formidable intellects to stop someone who they see as vulnerable from disclosing feelings or difficult experiences in their past. Sometimes they take it upon themselves to remind me of the risks of what I am opening up. They may be angry with me, doubting my competence or the capacity of the class to contain these feelings. In short, they both project their own need to manage emotions onto others and also overestimate the need that others have to be protected or rescued. They are often motivated to make things safe, shutting down difficult but pivotal learning.

A second challenge is also about emotion but refers to their own emotional life and difficulties with authorising themselves to feel, and to recognise feelings as valid and important cues. Many of the medically trained leaders I have worked with drive themselves so hard, and are so identified with their technical expertise, that they have lost the capacity to feel, and say, what matters to them. For some, this denial of feelings has been a necessary survival strategy, reinforced in professional life when they may routinely deal with tragedy. They may have been subject to intense 'baptisms of fire' as interns where the only way to survive is to withdraw emotionally. These very understandable coping mechanisms, however, bring problems for leadership.

In leadership roles, these medically trained individuals typically initially apply their intellectual and cognitive capacities, their work energy and appetite, to the job. Yet often these relied-upon aspects of their identity don't get them very far, especially in those roles which involve changing medical and hospital practices and cultures. Our work in class is focused on helping these medical leaders see that only drawing on their cognitive suite of skills—their 'smarts'—may leave others impressed, but unmoved. Part of the class work is about helping them to understand the processes by which they have put to bed their own emotions, only allowing them to surface in intimate relationships, not in leadership. Part of it is about seeing what they lose in this 'deal' they have made with themselves. The poignant insights often come first in relation to personal lives. What they eventually volunteer are comments such as: 'What I would really like is to allow myself time and space to find a partner'; 'My wife says her husband has returned'.

Next, the process can open up some greater freedom in their professional work: a recognition that while career success is important, so is their own happiness and health. In some cases, they also recognise that they have available to them many other less effortful but often more influential ways of doing the work, which involves giving attention to feelings.

For those who are very strongly identified with technical skills, one way to allow emotions in is through the lens of patient or customer needs. This step involves recognising that delivering good patient or customer service is not just about the technical quality or knowledge that leaders bring but about building a relationship which will outlive the intervention and help patients and clients take responsibility for ongoing changes that they need to make.

Because leadership is relational—it's about what goes on between people—emotions and feelings are almost always present, though rarely acknowledged. In their very useful book *Difficult Conversations*, Douglas Stone and his co-authors point out that most important, and difficult, conversations are about feelings. If they are not surfaced, those feelings remain to explode, to be repressed and result in disabling disconnection, or to stew in cynicism or sarcasm.

As I described earlier in the discussion of Tracy Castelino's work in domestic violence, intense and difficult feelings are often *the* central element of leadership work. They are not a side-effect of leadership actions. Acknowledging, shaping and directing feelings *is* the work.

When Christine Nixon assumed the role of Victoria's Chief Police Commissioner in 2004, she began to see data and hear evidence that domestic violence was a big and growing part of police work. Yet, at that time, it wasn't on the government or community agenda as a priority. Police officers felt ill-equipped to deal with it: 'We're not social workers,' they protested. The courts and court system meant that women who chose to charge or make a complaint against perpetrators were often subject to further abuse and undermining through the process of legal investigation and questioning. Christine asked herself and colleagues how she, and the police, could mobilise political and community attention on such a difficult issue—one that was accounting for more deaths and injury than road deaths and also causing more deaths than widely publicised diseases such as cancer. She wondered how to get the police, government departments and the Victorian government to begin recognising the scale of, and acting on, domestic violence.

Nixon and her senior colleagues at Victoria Police set about working with a wide range of stakeholders, including women's refuges, researchers and the court system. Interestingly, she targeted women politicians and senior public servants on both sides of politics.[1] However, the particular leadership initiative that she undertook which I want to focus on in this chapter was to mobilise police *feelings* about domestic violence in order to empower them to deal with it better. How did Nixon do this? A woman had written personally to Christine to tell her about the chronic, sustained abuse she had suffered at the hands of her partner and then at the hands of the police departments and courts when she tried to get assistance. Christine met with the woman and heard her powerful story. She was so moved by it that she asked whether the woman would be prepared to have it recorded and shown to police officers and people in the court system.

Christine's view was that many of those delivering services to victims of domestic violence had become inured to, and disconnected from, the pain and suffering involved in domestic violence. Although shutting off their feelings was sometimes an understandable response to dealing with these crises, in another sense these responses were holding back necessary change in ways of dealing with victims. As Christine saw it, those in the police and judicial system delivering services to victims had to be reminded what it felt like to be in the shoes of a domestic violence victim, with all the terror, shame and feelings of power-lessness that go along with long-term abuse.

Christine had a short film made, in which this victim of domestic violence talks candidly about what she has suffered. Listening to this woman talk is harrowing and deeply moving. She combats very simply some of the responses that are often faced by victims of domestic violence, such as, 'Why didn't you just leave?' This is an example of a situation where the leadership challenge involves mobilising feelings, as well as resources and programs. Christine and her colleagues saw an opportunity— the approach the victim made to tell her story—and used the emotive vehicle of a film of her talking to lead change.

As I write this now in 2015, there have been substantial

changes in political and public awareness of domestic violence and in resourcing to agencies involved in dealing with it. Senior police in Victoria, and more widely in Australia, now talk openly about the incidence and impact of domestic violence and take responsibility for occasions when police responses have failed. Police now work closely with community organisations; they measure and praise an increase in reporting of domestic violence. These changes, partially at least, stem from the leadership of Christine and others, such as 2015 Australian of the Year and victim of domestic violence herself Rosie Batty, which have been aimed at having workers like police and legal case workers truly feel for the plight of their clients, with a resulting drive to prevent violence rather than ignore it in future.

In leadership theory and in popular understandings of what it takes to be a leader, feelings and emotions have been seen as something to be got rid of, suppressed or sequestered into private lives. Yet increasing research indicates that there is a business and leadership 'case' for incorporating feelings such as compassion.

One source of emerging evidence is the work of Stanford University's Center for Compassion and Altruism Research and Education. Starting in around 2007, neurosurgeon James Doty and colleagues were interested in fostering and researching the impact of compassion in organisations. A key initiative was the development of Compassion Cultivation Training (CCT), an eight-week program of study which invites participants from all kinds of backgrounds. Based on the hypothesis that compassion could be encouraged through regular practical exercises, the team has also gathered extensive evidence on the effects of the training on participants—their physical and emotional well-being as well as how it affects their lives and work.[2] One participant, a doctor, describes how she felt near to breaking point before undertaking the training. Seeing up to 35 patients a day, they started to become just numbers to her and she stopped connecting to them. After the training in compassion, she used simple techniques, such as taking three deep breaths and mentally not carrying with her the last patient as she began with each new patient. She reported a number of effects. She got better at just giving each new patient her full attention, each current patient began to matter, and she realised, very power-fully, that she could offer caring in the moment as well as or instead of a prescription. At a more personal level, she admits that while her job is still very busy, she experiences less stress and feels a renewed sense of commitment and meaning in being a doctor.

Researchers in the field of emotional intelligence, such as Daniel Goleman, have done valuable work showing that how attuned leaders are to their own and others' emotions is more critical to their effectiveness than their cognitive intelligence. The importance of emotional intelligence in leadership is now well understood and involves capabilities including self-awareness, self-regulation of emotion, being alert to the emotional cues of others, and being skilful in interpreting feelings of others and expressing our own emotions.

Yet I want to add a mindful caveat to the emotional intelli-gence argument which has sometimes been distorted by popular prescription. I also want to offer some other reasons as to why and how emotions matter in leadership. Emotional intelligence and the capacity to regulate emotions should not simply be used to deliver a better leadership performance or to be rewarded as a 'people person'. When emotions are used instrumentally, as a means to some other goal, such as getting more productivity out of people, the goal remains unquestioned. Emotional management thus becomes another tool to reinforce a hierarchy and to enable leaders to get others to do what they want. Because of its calculated, instru-mental purpose, this use of emotions is remote from compassion or mindfully giving attention to other people's feelings.

Researcher Arlie Hochschild has had a long-term interest in studying how 'emotion management' can have profound consequences for employees who are continually required to deliver forced emotional performances, for example, of caring and nurturing. Hochschild's landmark study, *The Managed Heart*, showed the impact of emotional management and emotional labour on women air stewards.[3] Hochschild and subsequent researchers have shown that emotional labour is often done by women, young workers and others with little power, such as employees in child care, fast-food outlets and call centres. The risk, then, is that different rules of emotion management apply depending on where you are in an organisation and how much power you have. Those at the top can demonstrate shows of aggression and anger without consequence; indeed, the display of these emotions by men is sometimes interpreted as evidence of a necessary toughness in leadership. For those at the bottom or on the edge, the rules of emotional display are differently, yet more rigidly, prescribed. Failure to deliver the requisite emotions then meets with tough sanctions, as the research on call centres and lower status 'caring' work shows.

That leaders should give attention to their own and others' feelings is indispensable. But in doing so they should also be mindful of the hierarchical structures and power relations within which they are operating. Leading mindfully thus includes deep consideration of our purpose and intention, as well as the way our own 'stuff' can enhance, or get in the way of, leadership. These are subjects to which I turn in the next chapters.

Seventeen

BEING OURSELVES?

*Compassion and kindness frees us from the strangling
confines of self-involvement.*
Thupten Jinpa

Leaders aspiring to improve their effectiveness are sometimes
advised to be authentic or 'just be yourself!' What does this
advice mean, where does it come from and is it helpful in leading
mindfully? Here, I build on earlier discussion of leadership
reflection and identity work in Chapter 5 to suggest that mindfulness offers alternative insights about what to do with the self.
Being ourselves *less*, not more, may be a path that allows leaders
to be less ego-absorbed and frees them to give attention to the
needs of others and the challenges presenting themselves.

One of the most widely researched areas of leadership in the
last decade has been in authentic leadership, often seen as part
of transformational and charismatic leadership. This research
shows that recognised features of authenticity, such as the
following, are typically valued in leaders:

- self-awareness, evidence of reflection, owning one's own
  experiences and values, learning from life stories

- authentic behaviour: acting in accordance to values, consistency between words and deeds
- being able to hear, reflect and take account of our own and others' perspectives in a balanced way
- disclosure, being open to feedback and learning, able to risk vulnerability by revealing our own emotions.

Encouraging people to be honest, whole and grounded in their leadership, rather than feeling as though they must perform to an organisational template, is surely a welcome idea. My MBA students are often hungry for, and seize upon, the leadership solution of bringing your 'authentic self' to the table. Among seasoned leaders, authenticity is also an attractive ideal. There are three key reasons.

First, authenticity is a valuable aspiration because it has connections to integrity, honesty and being straight with people. In a world where so much of leadership seems to be about dissembling and spin, authenticity orients itself towards something more ethical and enduring.

Second, experiences shows that authenticity is welcomed by followers. Where the potential for an authentic relationship is present, it helps those working around and for leaders to trust and respect, it reminds them about their own values and purposes, and it supports and inspires them to face and tackle important challenges.

The third reason why authenticity is often recognised as worthwhile to aim for in leadership is the evidence that many people—especially, but not only, women and those from diverse racial and cultural backgrounds—want to do leadership differently. They feel pressure to conform to dominant norms about what leaders should look like, but they want to exercise leadership in ways that has more of themselves, with the values, life experiences and bodies that they bring. They understand that to perform to this dominant standard often involves a high level of 'management', including, for example, camouflaging bodies and suppressing feelings (this is not to say that men are not also subject to these processes but decades of evidence indicate it is more so for women[1]).

Authenticity can thus be a useful guiding value for those leaders who want to enact some transparency, who want to be present for those around them, perhaps also doing leadership in a way that captures some deeply held convictions about who they are and how they want to make a difference.

Yet aiming for authenticity as a leadership 'fix' is also full of problems. If we are interested in being mindful and present, authenticity might be a deviation. The first problem with advocating leaders be authentic is that the remedy fails to recognise that authenticity is not something an individual has. Authenticity is constructed in the interactions between leaders and followers. It is an assessment made about an attribute, not the attribute itself. Our judgements of who seems authentic to us are thus made through multiple, usually unconsciously held, lenses of cultural, gender and other stereotypes. Processes of judging who is authentic are fast and intuitive, not deliberatively considered, yet they directly inform assessments of trustworthiness and authenticity.

So, for some leaders, enacting an authentic self in leadership is relatively unproblematic because the look of them conforms to socially and culturally defined notions of trustworthiness and respectability. As described by Malcolm Gladwell and discussed in Chapter 12 'Looking after bodies', this is a well-documented effect. A tall, able-bodied, white and attractive male—think former US president Bill Clinton—who shares a story of recognisable struggle then achievement with appropriate humility, is likely to be judged perhaps as wrong-doing but also as authentic. Various sporting heroes—football, tennis and cricket players who occupy leadership roles—fit this pattern. But so also did initially feted and then disgraced cyclist Lance Armstrong. The point is that we are 'primed' to attribute authenticity to some leaders, until we discover damning evidence to the contrary.

When we turn to leaders of different gender or racial backgrounds, it's a different authenticity appraisal process. As I have explored in some of my other writing, female political leaders, such as Julia Gillard, Hillary Clinton or even Angela Merkel, are often assessed for authenticity on the basis of their bodies and gender—how they are seen as women—rather than assessed for what they do or say as leaders. Women in senior positions are routinely scrutinised according to their bodies, clothes, demeanour and sexuality as women. While they may be seen as authentic, that performance is more likely to be judged as antithetical to good leadership.[2] What is seen as touchingly authentic behaviour by a man, such as Bill Clinton's tears and remorse about his sexual relationship with Monica Lewinsky, is judged as inappropriately confessional or weak when exhibited by a woman. Even when senior women are judged as equally competent as male colleagues, research shows they are typically penalised for their success and considered 'less likeable'. Leadership authenticity is thus co-produced and not outside gendered norms and stereotypes.

The process of performing as and being judged an authentic leader is not nearly as simple as many authenticity gurus preach (and, interestingly, the authentic leadership literature is dominated by white male researchers).[3] Yet leaders are increasingly likely to be advised that they need to 'be themselves'. This is not just a simple matter of telling a few stories about the hardships endured in childhood. Social media and marketing gurus encourage leaders to craft their personal brand, then upload 'selfies'—evidence of their smart, quirky, endearing and lovable selves. In the case of former Australian Prime Minister

Kevin Rudd, or the situation where the world's presidents and prime ministers were captured on media taking selfies at the funeral of Nelson Mandela, there are many risks in being seen to be overly eager participants in self-image crafting, or unseemly self-promotion, even in the interests of being 'more authentic'.

My own experience as an academic provided some important learning for me around identity and authenticity. I thought for quite a while in my early career that I had to be the kind of academic who combines some version of the following: successful, funny and engaging teacher; wise and internationally respected professor; fearless defender of academic values and so on. As critical theorist Jo Brewis notes, our efforts to work at a self, even if it is an authentic self, may maintain an identity edifice that is in no-one's interest, neither the individual nor those around them: 'We commit ourselves to a particular version of self, giving us a platform from which to think and act, and we simultaneously begin to reject anything that does not conform to that self.'[4] As explored in earlier chapters, the mind then goes to work adding further beliefs and convictions that have a false solidity. They are 'what *I* believe in' and 'what *I* stand for', which then require defending and mean that other non-conforming but important phenomena are not seen or heard.

The second reason to be wary of advice to 'be oneself' or 'be authentic' in leadership is, in my view, even more compelling. Becoming engrossed in self and assuming that there is an enduring, separate self that we must work hard to uphold and protect, in my experience, causes suffering for leaders and often gets in the way of them doing valuable leadership work. The very search for authenticity may hook us into a self-preoccupation that is neither necessary nor an effective support to what we want to do in leadership and life.

SETTING ASIDE THE HUNGER FOR SELF

Social and cultural theory, as well as many other areas of scholarship, have extensively explored and critiqued contemporary Western society's glorification of, and obsessions with, self. As discussed in Chapter 5 'Reflecting on identity with less ego', diverse bodies of wisdom help us understand that the very notion of the independent self is a construction that we create and then shore up with our mind. While from a psychological point of view the process of identity formation is a crucial developmental task and a foundational platform for well-being, mindfulness encourages us to observe those identity formation urges and not just be captive in them.[5] For example, we might notice when our minds become colonised with thoughts about the injured or misjudged self and our efforts to defend it. In Buddhism, the remedy for this deeply human desire to *be somebody*, rather than a nobody, is to simply keep noticing it and then noticing that there is no real foundation for this belief. We create ourselves, with needs, responsibilities, things owed to us, earned by us. But these are all productions of our mind, and to recognise this can often bring enormous release, freedom and courage for leaders.

Tibetan teacher Sogyal Rinpoche says he offers what he hopes will be valuable teachings but he doesn't worry about what other people think. A friend of mine founded and built a highly successful construction business in his early career. It was so successful that he was able to extricate himself and live comfortably from his late 40s. He still works hard, contributes to the industry and community, and mentors young people, but he doesn't accept any payment for these activities. For him, this frees him from worrying about how people judge who he is and what he says and does, enabling him to follow more of his own moral compass.

Research and our own experience tells us that we are multiple selves. We adopt different personas for different contexts. Problems arise for leaders when they feel compelled to adopt masks in order to perform their jobs. No wonder, then, the attraction of notions of leadership authenticity. As followers we don't want to interact with masks, people who offer disingenuous faces that can't be trusted or relied upon.

Yet authenticity offers an overly simplified remedy in my view. While there may be some circumstances when it is helpful to others for us to hear and see heartfelt enactments of what matters to us, giving one's self too much solidity can sometimes hold us in approval-seeking, failure-avoiding, anxiety-reducing and control-maximising spaces.

Leading mindfully, then, may be less about you than about what happens *through you.* My wise and dear friend Richard Searle reminds me of this. What this insight means to me is that it's good to be ourselves lightly, with openness and presence, but without too much vested in our views or needs. The real identity task in leadership, I've suggested, is to step back from the drive to enact ourselves or perhaps inflict ourselves mindlessly on others. 'Being me' takes up energy and attention while I seek to make sure I come across in the right way, or alternatively descend into a cycle of self-recrimination when it doesn't all go to plan. In contrast, mindfulness gives us ways of pausing and noticing when the need to be someone stops us from really being here and now.

Eighteen

CLARIFYING PURPOSE, GOING FOR HAPPINESS

*It has been everywhere my happiness . . . but it was such
a small, plain thing that I mistook it for something ordinary
and failed to see.*
Rachel Joyce

The Dalai Lama—one of the world's most respected leaders—
says that the purpose of life is to be happy. Let that sit with you
for a moment . . .

It's a radical notion, isn't it? That we could orient our lives
and energies to helping promote our own and others' happiness.
I remember clearly the first time I read this simple statement by
the Dalai Lama. I felt an overwhelming sense of relief that it
was okay to want happiness for oneself—it doesn't mean we
are selfish, or weak, to seek this in our lives. I rang my mother
and we had one of those conversations that one is sometimes
blessed with: deep and profound, with her struggling to hear
why this was so powerful for me and me working to hear why
it might be so foreign to someone raised to believe the goals of
life lay in hard work, self-sufficiency, ideas and mental mastery.
I heard her grapple with the idea that although suffering (of

which she had experienced a lot) is part of the human condition, we can also 'go after' happiness.

It's potentially a deeply humanising idea, too. One of the practices which the Dalai Lama also recommends, and which I have followed over the years, is to spend a few moments when you wake up reminding yourself that everyone on earth wants to be loved and to be happy. The practice suggests you can bring people to mind, including those who may be causing you difficulty or grief, and simply remind yourself that they, too, want to be happy and to be loved.[1] Keep it simple, the Dalai Lama advises. Breathing in, cherishing yourself, and breathing out, cherishing others.

There are possibly all sorts of thoughts that may have arisen for you by reading the above paragraphs. The search for happiness, like authenticity, has become banal, so over-prescribed, over-conferenced and turned into 'tips for living' that many of us now experience the idea as trite and elusive. Your first reaction to the above might have been cynicism. Or you might have thought, 'It's not that simple!' or 'What if pursuing my happiness means I'm exploiting or hurting others?' Or you might have thought as I did, when I began engaging with this idea: 'But my job is to work hard, to get things done, to look after my family, to get good food on the table, to be there for my students, and so on . . . I haven't got time to go after my own happiness!' These are all understandable responses.

BEING CONNECTED TO PURPOSE

But I do want to suggest in this chapter that exploring purpose, including the opportunities that life and leadership present, to find happiness and enjoyment is a very good thing for leaders to do. Considering life's purpose invites us to stop seeing life as something to be got through. It makes us stop delaying enjoyment and postponing pleasurable life until circumstances get better. It helps us realise how precious human life is.

For leaders, it also is a very useful reminder of 'the big picture', asking ourselves, what are we here to do? What is the contribution or difference we want to make? In my experience, a common problem that leaders encounter is feeling as though there is life (the enjoyable bit, on weekends and holidays, with family and friends, going for rides, walks, travel, eating delicious food) and there is work (the long hours, the rigours of the job, the difficult people, the impossible targets). In groups of academic leaders I have worked with, the refrain goes something like:

> I'm just hanging out for end of term/sabbatical/long service leave/ the international conference in Prague/next year when I stop being head of department, and then it will be great . . . I'll get more time to do some research/writing/work with colleagues and then I'll be happy/spend time with the family/go back to exercise.

Frustratingly, no matter how well we plan, next year pans out to be as busy as this one.

Contemplating purpose is one antidote to these patterns of thinking which put life and current reality on hold. Being more connected to purpose can help leaders in several ways. First, it can insert a pause or at least give us perspective on the mental cycle described above. Hanging out for a different way of being, which somehow never arrives, leaves us full of sadness and disappointment. The recognition of the pattern can help us say to ourselves, 'Well, perhaps I can experiment with being present and enjoying life now.' In my coaching work, I often encourage clients to notice, and then shift, from a customary feelings of dread or being overwhelmed by an upcoming presentation or meeting, to inviting the possibility of enjoying it. The benefits of

offering this different kind of presence—open to the precious-
ness and value of life now—are felt by leaders and those working
with and for them. Leaders themselves feel less resentful and
overburdened about the circumstances of their work. Others
working with them can feel a freshness and invigoration, even in
the most challenging work.

A second set of benefits that may flow from an exploration of
purpose is that it can support leaders to be bold and courageous.
As discussed in Chapter 15, being bold and courageous surely
means being clear-sighted and prepared to stand up for important values, such as how we treat each other as people, or value
life in all its forms. It means not staying silent or going with
the crowd when those values have been breached or lost sight
of. Unfortunately, my own research reveals that often, among
leaders, physical bravery, toughness, stamina and endurance get
confused as markers of courage. It seems routine now for high-
achieving leaders to also be marathon athletes or mountain
climbers aiming to go beyond base camp.[2] I'll never forget the
words of a senior manager I was coaching who said that when
he was given a terminal diagnosis, he wished someone had urged
him to relinquish the prior, physically demanding goals he set
for himself. The physical endurance goal was just not the important one any more, and he needed someone to remind him of
that. There is nothing at all wrong with being fit as a leader—
it's a good thing—but there is something wrong with equating
courage, boldness and clarity of purpose with physical stereotypes of endurance or charisma.

My reason for dwelling on this is that while my experience is
that exploring values and purpose—what kind of difference we
want to bring in our leadership—is very valuable to many leaders,
some of us come under pressure to deliver a particular (sometimes gendered) performance of purpose. We can feel pressured
that we must adopt a 'mission' or 'purpose' that is overly grand or

impressive. The leadership literature and the popular discourses that accompany it can exacerbate this problem, telling us we've got to go for greatness. Nothing less than global transformation—being an iGod of innovation like Steve Jobs—will do!

My own purpose, as I have come to understand it, is to love and help others find some freedom for themselves. It feels difficult to say that, to put it down in words on this page, and I'm sure there are lots of people I've interacted with who would reply, 'Well, you got that wrong with me, honey! I didn't feel much love or freedom in your presence!' or 'What sentimental rubbish.' Undoubtedly some are right. Not all of my actions accomplish this purpose. However, it has been a way for me to sort things out, to decide where to place my energies and how to let other things go. It provides fail-safe criterion to know what I go the extra mile for.

I first came across Gordon Cairns, now Chair of Origin Energy, Woolworths and a Champion of Change[3] in gender equality, when he was CEO of Lion Nathan in the late 1990s. My friend Valerie Wilson and I were seeking to understand what made for effective leaders of diversity. We interviewed CEOs who had a reputation for managing diversity and cross-cultural issues well, and who were often the product of diverse, cross-cultural or what we called 'boundary-crossing' experiences themselves.[4] These leaders 'got' the experience of being different. They brought courage and conviction to the idea that people should not be pressured to conform to traditional templates of leadership. Gordon didn't necessarily feel a traditional leader himself, though he was a very effective one when measured against conventional business metrics. But he did see, often in his wider leadership work and with his male senior peers in the business community, many examples where the contribution of outstanding aspiring leaders was lost because they were not seen as conforming to the leadership template—for example, they got pregnant ('how inconvenient') or they wanted to put a value on family life.

Later, Gordon and I came to know each other better as part of our shared interest in mindfulness, Buddhism and leadership. Gordon is one of the founding members, along with Diane Grady, David White and others, who convened a Leaders' Retreat, an annual gathering of Australian business leaders for a two-day program of teachings, discussion and meditation with Buddhist teacher Sogyal Rinpoche. Rinpoche is the author of *The Tibetan Book of Living and Dying*, for me among the most truly valuable books I have ever read (and continue to re-read), offering practical insight on how to live and die well.

Although initially Gordon kept some of his private journey in exploring Buddhism and spirituality separate from his business life, increasingly he has been explicit that the *dharma* (or teachings) and business are, or should be, about the same things. They are about how to create cultures that are tough on issues and compassionate with people; that effective organisational cultures are nurtured not just on results but how we get them; that we must inhabit the moment, living each day fully and as if it might be your last; that we are not two people—the organisational leader and the private person—but one, with a common value set; and that we must pay attention to how people are feeling as well as what they think. In Buddhism, the heart and the mind are one thing, not two, and cultivating *bodhichitta* (compassion) is a powerful basis for business leadership.

I have included a description of Gordon's leadership in the context of purpose and courage because I think he provides an example of a respected business leader who has been unafraid to be vulnerable, share himself and his failings, to take risks and to change. In fact, one of the key requisites of leadership in his view is that we should be open to coaching and deep change ourselves. Gordon provides a model of this himself, describing the processes by which he has had to hear and grapple with confronting feedback. He offers a message of humanity: listen to what people and your family tell you—especially the difficult stuff—and learn from it; don't work to a predefined set of goals or single-mindedly pursue career success if it means unhappiness for those who matter most to you; meet fear and anger with as much loving kindness as you can muster.[5] In his speech on leaving Lion Nathan after eight years as its CEO, he identified the collective creation of a culture and a 'soul . . . emotional, spiritual and immortal' as especially precious to him:

> We create meaning in our life by finding meaning in our work, and in our selves. We learn to love others as we would ourselves, and sometimes we have to learn to accept the unbearable in delivering them bad news . . . This soul makes us special. It is our strongest competitive weapon, unseen, all powerful, not capable of imitation or copy.

How have these approaches accrued benefits in Gordon's leadership? In his years as Australian CEO of Lion Nathan, until he stepped down in 2006, the company went from declining earnings and market share, with high management turnover and poor morale, to top quartile financial performance, increasing market share and the award of one of Australia's most admired companies for three consecutive years. He is first to point out this was a team performance, not the result of individual leadership. However, his own role in creating a different culture is undeniable, beginning with asking for feedback and determining to change in response to it. The Lion Nathan values that the organisation set about clarifying were not grandiose or, on the other hand, pious (it is an alcoholic drinks company, after all). They included passion, helping each other, being sociable, facing reality and acting with integrity.

Gordon has continued to exercise leadership in his later career as a non-executive director, for example, as Chair of Origin Energy. His outspokenness on gender inequalities, and arguing that it is men who must name and take responsibility for change, has led him to be an influential member of former and pioneering Sex Discrimination Commissioner Elizabeth Broderick's group of male Champions of Change. Gordon mentors young managers, encourages others, including me, to keep true to our values, and he and his wife go on at least two long breaks a year to renourish, to walk the Camino de Santiago or learn about the ancient history of Uzbekistan. He is lucky and he knows it, but he also supports others to be bold and follow their heart. Gordon's experience is that in corporate life, a high-achieving culture and valuing people—and their desires to live a full and happy life—are not mutually exclusive. They are intimately connected, and shaping the circumstances which foster this union are a central part of what leaders are there for.

Nineteen

BEING ETHICAL

The most potent tool managers have in navigating difficult ethical territories is themselves—their bodies, hearts and minds.
Donna Ladkin

I began exploring the links between ethics, leadership and mindfulness some years ago when I was teaching a subject called Management and Ethics at Melbourne Business School. I am not philosophically trained and there are big gaps in my knowledge about the fine differences between utilitarianism and consequentialism, indeed how to define and differentiate ethics and morals. For the first few years I shared teaching the subject with classically trained philosophical colleagues who I enjoyed listening to and learning from. But I was not convinced then, and remain unconvinced, that there is necessarily a correlation between philosophical knowledge and ethics.

One of the reservations I have had about much of the business ethics literature, and ethics more broadly, is its orientation to the thinking mind and the intellect as the source of ethics. During my time teaching ethics, I did a lot of research seeking to understand philosophical perspectives such as the deep ecology movement and feminist ethics. Writers in these fields provide compelling critiques of ethics as it has often been taught, and argue for other perspectives and dimensions of experience to be given weight in understanding ethics. The deep ecologists, for example, argued for the earth and sentient species to be respected and valued for themselves, and not for how they can be used for human gain. Feminist and later post-colonial philosophers have questioned the use of concepts like 'human rights' as the fundamental scaffolding of ethical thinking. Rather than proceeding from the start point of allocating and protecting human rights, some of these theorists suggest ethics should start with understanding and seeking to minimise suffering. Some also advocate a pre-eminent ethical role for caring, a quality that had often been devalued in cognitively anchored models of ethics.

Despite (or perhaps because of) not covering much conventional philosophy, the course was very successful and enjoyable for me and my students. My hunch is that this was because we explored together: how we are with others, how to learn from each other and recognise the integrity of different histories and life experiences.

How might mindfulness contribute to a broader understanding of ethical capability, beyond philosophical knowledge? In an often-cited quote, nineteenth century psychologist William James said: 'The faculty of voluntarily bringing back a wandering attention over and over again, is the very root of judgement, character and will.' One of the ingredients of good judgement, James suggested, is not knowledge or expertise but the capacity to bring back 'wandering attention' to what is before and around us now. In research with lawyers and judges, legal scholars Lisle Baker and Daniel Brown find that making good judgements depends on summoning sharp attentional skills to the precise circumstances before us. They add that, ironically, this focusing of attention 'requires temporarily quieting the active process of elaborated thought that law students, lawyers and judges pride themselves on having developed as part of their legal education'.[1] To make ethical judgements, judicial leaders may need to be able to set to one side their usual habits such as diligent preparation, and instead substitute close attention to noticing what is emerging moment by moment. This new data may be of a different kind to what they are used to giving attention to, and it may require them to let go of some of their usual sense-making responses.

In the different context of teaching ethics to MBA students, leadership scholar Donna Ladkin also maintains that foundational ethical practices are less about knowledge and theoretical proficiency than about attention, noticing and asking good questions.[2] Default or even deliberative patterns of thinking and recourse to customary models may be antithetical to the self-reflective presence required for good ethics.

Decision-making researchers have explored the cognitive traps, the pre-existing categories, stereotypes, and convenient and well-used cognitive by-ways which our minds tend to travel along when facing difficult ethical decisions or unexpected information. For example, Nicole Reudy and Maurice Schweitzer argue that unethical decisions often stem from a lack of reflection and ability to be self-aware. In two separate but related studies, these researchers show that self-serving cognitive justifications, self-deception and unconscious biases were associated with low scores on mindfulness scales, and a greater propensity to engage in unethical conduct such as cheating. In contrast were those who rated high on mindfulness and were more likely to uphold ethical standards and adopt a principled approach to decision-making.

A further way in which mindfulness might build ethical capabilities is through cultivation of wisdom. Wisdom is typically distinguished from knowledge and it includes several emphases that will, by now, be familiar aspects of mindfulness. First, wisdom involves a capacity to observe and pay attention to reality, rather than prejudging or assuming. Thus wisdom includes using all the faculties, not just the cognitive, to arrive at an understanding of what is occurring and what might be an ethical way forward.

Everyone who comes to meditation and mindfulness does so with their own history and experiences. The relationship each of us finds between mindfulness and ethics may be different, and the path of exploration in itself changes us. Buddhists teach that one should not follow a path or adopt a practice just because we are told to. They advise us to always apply the test of our experience. A central part of the process which often unfolds is an exploration of values and ethics. In my experience, this exploration is far from the arcane philosophising that we sometimes associate with ethics. Mindfulness thus offers very practical ways of helping people stay grounded in reality and connected to what matters to them. It can help them notice when they get caught in excessive driving and striving which is not good for them or the people around them. This practically grounded ethics is welcomed by leaders, though it may not have the rather high-minded title of ethics. Introduced to mindfulness, many leaders make changes in the way they do things, in their careers or organisations, to better serve a purpose or set of values that may have become jeopardised. There are also ostensibly modest but consequential changes in how we live and how we are with others: for example, whether we experience gratitude with partners and make a commitment to listen and attend to their comments about us rather than act defensively.

Yet there are risks for those seeking to bring mindfulness into leadership. Because of its popularity, mindfulness is at risk of being treated as a fad or a 'fix' that allows other agendas to be masked.[3] We should be concerned if mindfulness is put to the wheels of global capitalism, enabling people to feel less stressed about doing immoral things, or in less obvious ways feeding exploitation, punishing work cultures or unsustainable materialism. An example are the concerns expressed about organisations such as the US military teaching mindfulness to combat soldiers whose job it is to crush the enemy. Further, while mindfulness initiatives are often led by well-intentioned people, organisations are full of contradictions. An enlightened 'brand' and reputation are sometimes then exploited. For example, running meditation or mindfulness programs for staff to ease the symptoms of stress can avoid addressing unsustainable or exploitative work practices, or divert attention from less savoury aspects of corporate business models such as aggressive tax minimisation or benefitting from very low labour conditions in off-shore suppliers. While head office or high-status employees might benefit from a focus on mindfulness, contracting and outsourcing mean that workers in far-flung locations suffer with less protection.

A further set of ethical risks is described by Buddhist writer Chögyam Trungpa in his book *Cutting Through Spiritual Materialism*. He explains that people are good at using spiritual insight to 'get somewhere' or display their own wisdom and superiority. He warns that the ego can turn anything—even a spiritual practice—to its own use. Both history and contemporary life are regrettably full of examples where spiritual leaders have done just that—told themselves that their spirituality or calling elevates them from the need to follow ordinary ethics. If we are interested in mindful leadership, we are seeking to notice when mindful practices get used to prop up ego and help us feel superior or self-satisfied.

To introduce mindfulness to make more money or improve competitive position or productivity leaves out a central, perhaps the most central, mindful teaching, which is about our intention. In his summary of The Five Mindfulness Trainings originally taught by the Buddha, Thich Nhat Hanh says that mindfulness includes a commitment to prevent suffering, and to prevent others from profiting from suffering or the suffering of other species.[4]

Yet Hanh also shows characteristic equanimity about some of these risks by arguing that if people engage genuinely in mindfulness then gradually a reorientation of purpose follows.[5] The evidence is that mindfulness is not a technique that can be decoupled from its intent and purpose.

Negotiating an ethical path in leadership is a life's learning and each of us will draw on different knowledge, experiences, habits of reflection and practices to support us along that path. Mindfulness offers some simple but powerful guide posts that are different from traditional approaches to ethics in leadership and business. My own experience is that mindfulness, in that simplicity and difference, is a very good companion to ethics.

In the previous chapter, I described how mindfulness had become a central underpinning of the leadership of Gordon Cairns. At the Mindful Leadership Global Forum in Sydney in 2014, he offered the following lessons from his experience about leading ethically:

- Notice your impact on others.
- Be grateful for feedback and advice, don't abuse people who tell you about reality.
- Ask for help: 'When the pupil is ready the teacher appears.'
- Look for purpose and meaning together with others.
- Be tough and clear-sighted on issues, be clear about reality.
- Pay attention to feelings, they are often a better guide than the so-called 'rational' mind.
- Be compassionate with people: when encountering anger and resentment, respond with loving kindness.

Twenty

BRINGING LOVE AND
COMPASSION INTO LEADERSHIP

We not only wanted to make them better players,
we wanted to make them better people.
That's what I see as mindfulness.
Paul Roos

Paul Roos is a successful Australian football coach, leading
the Sydney Swans to their first premiership in 2005, and more
recently moving to coach the Melbourne Demons.[1] Known not
just for his own success as a player and for coaching premier
teams, Roos is renowned for his different leadership approach:
his care for his players and his belief that they need to have
tools to perform well in life as well as sport. With his wife,
Tami Roos, who is a meditation teacher, Paul has instigated
programs where players in his previous and present football
clubs are taught meditation, just as they are taught about the
importance of a good diet and sleep. Paul says you need to
know players to help them. This includes understanding the
fears which can accompany them onto the football ground;
understanding the norms and pressures on them that often
equate masculinity with aggression; and helping them stay

focused while being put on a pedestal one game and dragged off it the next.

In working with the players, Tami Roos says:

> Players are no different than most individuals in that you sometimes have to guide them to practise self-love, and meditation is one of the greatest forms of self-love they can practise. Meditation teaches them the importance of looking after their minds, helps build resiliency and creates a space of time in their day that helps them recharge their batteries. A player may also need to be reminded of the importance of setting boundaries, getting a good night's sleep, learning how to prioritise . . . All of these are forms of practising self-love.[2]

In Paul Roos' leadership, love comes through in a variety of ways. It is there in the way he debriefs after a game, supporting improvement rather than running people down, and in the way he encourages players to put in effort as husbands and fathers. When asked about a player's form or about one who may be experiencing a form slump, Paul emphasises focusing on the player's strengths not his weaknesses, thus nurturing confidence through kindness and compassion. In interviews about the game's loyal supporters, he volunteers he has nothing but admiration for them because they ride the highs and lows of the footy club like the players and coaches, and they are one of the main reasons you have a footy club. There is nothing sentimental or soft about this leadership which emphasises love and compassion. It is direct, felt and leads to excellent outcomes for players and fans. What is perhaps remarkable and refreshing is Paul's willingness to talk about the centrality of love and compassion in what he does—the acknowledgement in itself is an act of leadership.

In this chapter I explore the possibilities of love in leadership. First, I consider some of the myths and reactions that can get in our way when exploring love in the context of leadership. I can hear dismay and cynicism in the reactions of some academic colleagues even as I write this chapter! Paul and Tami Roos likely encountered similar but perhaps more bluntly expressed responses from some players and supporters.

But it is worth persisting for many reasons—societies and organisations have developed many myths about leadership that deserve to be challenged. Some of us also harbour in ourselves beliefs about our own unlovability or shortcomings in being able to love that also deserve to be challenged. Most importantly, the evidence is that leadership is most inspiring and freeing when it comes from a place of love and compassion for others. Here, I draw on diverse research to show how love can be incorporated in leadership in ways that are practical and everyday, rather than mystical or rare.

MORE EXPANSIVE VIEWS OF LOVE

In most contemporary societies we have inherited, and live as if, there is a dichotomy between love and work. Love is for private lives. It is appropriately directed towards families, partners and friends. Most portrayals of love in movies, books and other media are usually only interested in romantic or sexual love. Love is portrayed as a lightning bolt—it either arrives in our lives in the form of another person or, sadly, does not. It is the key to our happiness but, significantly, largely out of our control.

This view of love, I suggest here, is deeply unhelpful for many reasons. It only recognises romantic love and it encourages passivity or at least resignation, implying we have nothing to do with whether love is present in our lives. Many philosophers have offered more useful explorations. Ancient Greek philosopher Socrates identified *storge* (familial love), *xenia* (a love for strangers), *philia* (the love in friendship) and *agape* (a more god-like love reflecting love of life and other beings) alongside the more familiar *eros* (sensuous, erotic love). European philosophers such as Michel de Montaigne and Johann Wolfgang von Goethe also explore the many permutations of love that are threaded through, indeed give meaning and purpose to, everything we do in life.[3]

Women writers from diverse traditions, including European philosophers, Simone de Beauvoir, Luce Irigaray and Hélène Cixous, alongside psychologists such as Jean Baker Miller and Carol Gilligan, have pointed to the neglect of love and caring in scholarship on knowledge-creation and moral development. Gilligan, for example, argues that the 'logic of justice' has been overvalued as a marker of ethical superiority. As discussed in the previous chapter, she and others have advocated an equally important basis for ethics which hinges on an ethic of care, of acting to minimise suffering.

Emerging neuroscientific evidence also gives us new and important perspectives on love. While neurobiology has been slow to investigate love and how it shapes the brain, research by psychologists working, for example, with children who have been neglected or abused shows that love changes both the brains of the person who loves and the one who is loved. Emotion largely arises from the 'middle' or limbic brain, a neural network that can be strengthened or weakened by experience, relationships and practice. Children who have not experienced much love are stunted in these particular areas of the brain. But those areas can be developed through later loving and caring relationships. Indeed, therapeutic interventions are designed to give the child repeated and genuine experiences of being cared for and loved. Neurological studies show that these positive relational interactions change their brains.[4]

So, although capacity to love is shaped most by early

experiences, it can be learned and expanded by practice. In further research on what are termed 'mirror neurons',[5] it has been demonstrated that people who express empathy and connection towards another can change and enrich the other's neural connections. Through the expression of love and care, another's neurobiology and neural structures can be changed in ways that affect their experience of life.

LOVE IN LEADERSHIP

The research summarised above encourages all of us interested in leadership to reconsider love—not as a high-minded ideal, applicable only to close family and friends, but potentially a practical part of leading well. What forms might this take?

In his book on leadership, the Dalai Lama suggests that 'it is the task of the leader to create a company with a strong and warm heart and to see things as they really are'.[6] I sometimes share this definition of leadership with groups, pausing to allow its impact to land. In this one statement, the Dalai Lama radically inverts our notions of leadership. First and foremost, he gives the leader responsibility for building a strong and warm heart. This task is clear, unsentimental and involves hard work. Love is understood to be the wish for happiness for others, while compassion is the wish for others to be free of suffering. To build a strong, warm heart involves diligently and persistently wishing for others—those one knows and likes, and those one doesn't— to escape suffering and to enjoy happiness. Another stunning and useful insight from Buddhism is that one can cultivate love for others without necessarily liking them. The other part of the leader's job description, from the Dalai Lama's perspective, is to see things as they are: to be mindful, present and not caught in illusion.

In an earlier chapter I referred to the work of Adam Kahane, a consultant who works with communities and policy-makers on implementing social change. Kahane draws on the writings and model of Martin Luther King, who maintained: 'Power at best is love implementing the demands of justice. And justice at its best is love correcting everything that stands against love.' Kahane argues that social-change leadership involves working with, and balancing, the twin forces of power and love. You need to harness power or the drive to self-realisation with the drive to connect and unite. Power used generatively makes love empowering instead of sentimental and anaemic. Love makes power unifying instead of reckless and abusive. Paul and Tami Roos' work with footballers provides an example of the two forces simultaneously engaged.

Kahane has observed that for both political and psychological reasons when we are under pressure we tend to revert to either power or love. He advises leaders to always keep both 'drives' in view and to refuse to choose between them. He encourages leaders to acknowledge and initiate discussion of questions like: 'Where is the power here?' 'Whose views are being heard?' 'How are actors separated and unified?' 'What are the sources of difference and conflict?' Further, and resonant with our earlier discussion on mindful dialogue, Kahane advises that groups cultivate their capability to tolerate difference and conflict, and resist premature or false consensus.

When I started doing teaching training in yoga, I thought I was learning about yoga and about how to teach it. As the course unfolded, I realised how much more was being made available: not just about how to teach—though certainly my whole approach as a teacher shifted—but about how to live and how to lead. A valuable yoga class is not about which physical postures one teaches in what order, but about deeper intent and impact: whether students leave feeling held and loved, recognised for who they are, cherished for the effort they have made to be there, and supported to keep going. Could I take these principles into a leading an MBA class? Could I stop worrying about getting through the content and love them instead? Quite a few disasters unfolded where I forgot that I also need to be clear and firm about reality! There were other classes where I lost or devalued the ideas and content that I know is practical and useful for people. Being soft, fudging things, allowing oneself to get hijacked and side-tracked is of no use to anyone, especially aspiring leaders who want to have a positive impact on the people around them.

A different example of the role of love in leadership comes from research of Indigenous and environmental leadership. Over the course of many years I have worked with my former PhD student Michelle Evans, who is an Indigenous artist and community development practitioner. Michelle arrived at my door, having worked with Indigenous artists and arts managers, with the hunch that, through their art practices, they were exercising leadership—for their own and the white Australian communities, for their ancestors and future generations, for their lands and their culture. Through Michelle's research, I have come to hear and observe how love of and respect for land and country, and its custodianship for future generations, is a driver of everything else in community leadership. For example, and as described by Bangarra Dance Theatre Director Stephen Page, 'The land shapes the people, the people shape the language, the language shapes the songs and the songs will then determine the dance and the spirit will be what it is.' In Page's view, land provides leadership and this can be felt through people's caretaking:

It's like the leadership is a spirit . . . really just accepting that the land has a strong spirit which is the leader. I think we forget that this land was chosen to have a great body of spirituality, a lot of precious spirituality. It's something that you can only feel and I think we try to bottle it up and we try to pigeonhole it and it's too spirited to be formed ... we shouldn't be afraid of the land's spirituality. That's what's been such a great gift to Aboriginal people ... that's what's been the challenge for Aboriginal people is the caretaking of that spirit—of the many, many spirits.

American environmental activist Naomi Klein writes similarly about the mobilising power of communities' deep love and connection with land and non-human species in her recent book *This Changes Everything.* She suggests that the most important global environmental campaigns are not anti-development but rather reflect the 'power of ferocious love' for lands and waters, for the capacity to continue custodianship.[7] In the examples that Klein cites, diverse communities talk about their connection to land. It is integral to individual and collective identity, and part of what they are here to do is look after it for future generations. Increasingly over recent decades, farmers in all parts of the world also talk about their identity and purpose rooted in love of the land and following practices that will not just preserve it but leave it in better condition than they found it.

Also going beyond the human realm, environmental philosophers and deep ecologists such as Joanna Macy say that love must be at the heart of our being in the physical world and 'inter-being' with non-human species. She advocates environmental activists lead by 'falling in love' with the world, and live with a 'wild love for the world'.[8] Macy distinguishes this sensuous, vibrant way of directly experiencing the world from human-centred ways of *thinking about* the world. In her view, human thinking often gets in the way, rendering us powerless or pessimistic. In contrast, Macy says, we are 'built' to take delight in what is around us, through our senses of sight, smell and touch. Our task is to be present to it, to welcome it with 'curiosity and gladness for the opportunity'. While this may sound like a hedonist's prescription, Macy believes this love for the world and its sacredness is the foundation for powerful activism.

OPENING OUR HEART AND CULTIVATING LOVE

In another of his superb little books, *True Love,* Thich Nhat Hanh provides deeply practical guidance about how to love more. To truly love another we must first understand them, he says. To do this, we give time to 'looking deeply' into the person, to be there, attentive, and to observe beneath the surface. According to Thich Nhat Hanh, there are four elements of love we can work on:

- *Maître* or loving kindness: not only the desire to make someone happy, but also the ability to bring joy and happiness to the loved person; it requires practice, cultivation of intention and action.
- *Karuna* or compassion: not only the desire to ease the suffering of another person, but the ability to do so. It requires practice in deep looking to understand the nature of the suffering of our loved one.
- *Mudita* or joy: if there is no joy in love, it is not true love.
- *Upeksha*, a special freedom: to practise loving in such a way that the person we love feels free, not only outside but also inside.

From this perspective, to love is to cultivate deep under-standing, achieved through 'deep looking' and deep listening; it is about being attentive and observant, intently present to others, and it is about action—practically alleviating suffering and offering support—not just expressing nice feelings. Finally, love needs to be joyful, and to have a result that is experienced as greater freedom.

In what might appear to be an unpromising context—an MBA classroom—researcher Steve Taylor invites his leadership students to '"open their heart" to their classmates'. He says, 'They all seem to know what that phrase means without any explanation from me.'[9] Taylor suggests that all of us have a sense about what is involved in opening our heart, and philosophical discussions don't add much. In leadership, opening our heart includes sharing a part of ourselves that others recognise as real and true. But it's not just telling the good bits or the situations where one triumphs over adversity (one of the problems with the common exhortation to be authentic). According to Taylor, opening our heart is a baring of aspects of self, a preparedness to be vulnerable, which often deepens the connection between ourselves and others. It involves sharing one's struggles in leadership, how one is not perfect and why it's difficult.

Encouraging his leadership students to experiment with opening their hearts, Taylor finds that the key obstacle is fear and assumptions developed early in life that allowing others to see our deeply flawed selves will mean they won't love, respect or follow us.[10] A particular problem for leaders is that they get caught up in the norms of leader-follower status games, which in turn prevent connection, collaboration and creativity. Rational argument doesn't get around these obstacles, which is why Taylor opens a distinctly different MBA space to work at a more physical level, including letting your feelings show. In this sense, letting feelings and vulnerability show and expressing love is also an invitation to others to love. As I was re-reading Taylor's moving chapter on opening your heart, I was reminded of Paul Roos and his apparently simple, but deeply powerful, leadership act, of modelling compassion and love for players, supporters and others with whom he is working.

My name—Amanda—means 'born to be loved'. Yet I spent much of my early life unsure whether I was lovable enough. I suspect these fears are not uncommon. I grew up at a time and in a household where self-reliance was valued and demonstrativeness frowned upon. The death of my father when I was fifteen sent me into the arms of numerous boyfriends, many of whom were sweet and well-meaning but not up to the job of loving me enough to satisfy my voracious, romance-fuelled longings. I experienced the break-up of my first marriage when I had two young children. I spent a lot of time listening to— perhaps wallowing in is more accurate—a song by Madonna called 'Love Don't Live Here Anymore'. The lyrics were written about me, I was sure and, feeling abandoned by love, I waited for it to arrive in my life. It wasn't until later that I could see it was there all through that time in my children, my mum and brother, my friends and then my new partner.

Sometimes I have felt very daunted by the enormous good done by others. My own positive influence can seem very circumscribed by comparison. Rather tough on myself around this issue, I believed that my job was to love others more. I brought all my strongly driven conscientiousness to the task! However, I have noticed in experimenting with, for example, expanding feelings and actions of love towards others, that it doesn't take much to have a palpable impact for them, to visibly relieve suffering. Now, lots of things keep reminding me about love's power: people arrive at my door, grandchildren appear and relationships deepen, the standoffish cat finally sits on my lap. Since I started thinking about love, I notice its presence more—in relationships, even in fleeting encounters between strangers in a train carriage or supermarket queue.

As part of giving a series of teachings in Mexico in 2013, the Dalai Lama directly reassured those of us who might be doubtful of our capacity to make a big difference to others by cultivating a warm heart.[11] He said:

Each of us has the potential to express human values in our own lives. We can develop a sense of warm-heartedness ourselves, pass it on to our children, and cultivate it within our family. We can extend it to other families in our neighbourhood so it spreads like a ripple effect across a lake.

Buddhist teacher Ayya Khema says, 'To look for love is a totally unsatisfactory endeavour and will never be satisfying. It sometimes works and sometimes doesn't. That which does work is to love.'[12] In the Buddhist view, we all have a vast and natural capacity to love. It's not a matter of learning or re-learning how to love. It's a matter of removing the 'obscurations', the things that get in the way of us remembering the central truth of love, relinquishing the defences we've learned that stop us from getting in touch with our natural ability to love and to be lovable—just as we are.

Acknowledgements

A YEAR OF DELIGHTS
AND LETTING GO

After a lot of prevaricating (that's a word my mum used to use, and despite my kids quibbling about how it's different from procrastinating, I'm attached to it), then saying to myself and others 'the world doesn't need another leadership book' (which is true), towards the end of 2014 I allowed myself to begin writing this book. At first it was just notes from my reading and research. Increasingly, I added experiences and insights from coaching and running leadership programs that felt important. Individuals that I'd worked with sent emails like 'I feel like a weight has been lifted from me and am much happier' and 'Thank you for a great session. I really enjoyed your way of handling a pretty cynical bunch without compromising your own values'. A senior woman doctor came to me at the end of a half day on leading mindfully and eyeballed me. She'd been a quietly challenging member of the group so I wasn't sure what was coming: 'This is essential to me surviving' was what she said. 'Learning to do more of this (mindfulness) is what will keep me alive.'

The 200 or so Masters of Public Health students at Melbourne University I present to annually on Leadership and Mindfulness are also always a delight. I rarely teach such a rich diversity—of age, cultural background and public health roles. I only have them for an hour and a half but there are powerful experiences 'in the moment' of the class and in the conversations that follow. One emergency doctor introduced herself to me at the end of the class saying that she looks after lots of people, many with catastrophic injuries and near death. She shared that there is little time in these literally life-or-death situations, but the one thing that all people want is for you to listen to them, not treat them as a body or set of body readings. In another case, I heard from the Masters of Health Program Director about one mature-age student who had shared in the class exercises on mindfulness, his very difficult relationship with his estranged son, and his sorrow about this. That man had then walked out of the class and bumped into his son in the street outside. Partially because of our work in class, he was able to initiate a new and open reconnection with his son. Another young man who talked to me after the last group I taught came to Australia from Vietnam on his own as a refugee at sixteen. We had a beautiful exchange and moment of connection lasting only perhaps five minutes that then, and now, lifts my heart. I want to similarly acknowledge and thank participants of many programs and classes for sharing your experiences and being open to learning about leading mindfully. You know who you are!

There are particular individuals I want to thank for their support. I feel that support physically even though some of you live very far away. Richard Searle, Emma Bell and Donna Ladkin, thank you for your encouragement to write this book and for your ongoing friendship and love. To others, especially inspiring leader Christine Nixon, thank you for our work together. You've taught me so much about the value of partnering, about being open to and enjoying what each new group brings. Jean-Alain D'Argent and the Dharma Yoga community have been wonderful companions along the mindfulness journey. Thank you to David White and others at Rigpa for organising for the annual Sogyal Rinpoche Leaders' Retreat. Rinpoche's presence has the profound effect of eliciting 'calm abiding'. What a gift.

Lest you think it's been one gorgeous teaching experience after another, I have had some blistering experiences too when everything I've learned about letting go of ego and my desire to be loved have been put to the test. Some MBA students have been really cross with my content, assessment and most other things about me. One young woman whispered tentatively to me at the end of one program, 'I hope this group doesn't find its way into your next book as an example of difficult groups with hostile responses'. Well, here you are! But even amidst these very testing experiences, there were heartfelt responses in this group too. As the Dalai Lama says, you learn most from the people who cause you most suffering.

So, this book owes most to you all—students, participants of programs and people I've coached and those I've befriended, the many I've been moved and inspired by, the ones I've mentioned in the book and the ones I haven't. The ones who've pushed me hard with cynicism, irritation, even fury at wasting their energies, so hard that I really had to identify and let go of the residual ego and need to be liked that was getting in the way of my own leadership.

I wanted to include in *Leading Mindfully* stories and anecdotes from real leaders, who are practising mindfulness in their work and who have inspired me. Thank you to all of you who have agreed to be identified in this book. When I sent out drafts, I hoped you wouldn't be too horrified at what I'd written about you and you haven't! Allen & Unwin publisher Elizabeth Weiss and her team have been rock-like in their support of this project. Elizabeth is a mindfulness practitioner herself and her knowledge and wise counsel about how to bring these ideas to a wide audience has been incredibly valuable, despite my protestations at times.

On the home front, the delights have been and continue to be many. Charlie must be the most sweet-tempered year 12 student ever, so tolerant of his mum's absentmindedness and her undoubtedly poorly informed views on micro-economics. Charlie's trumpet playing has filled our house and lives with fantastic jazz—played by Charlie and his school mates as well as other greats—what a joy that's been. As life is wont to offer there have been births and deaths in the year of writing this book. Julie, my oldest friend and a staunch defender of me and all things common sense in the Beaumaris Primary school yard, died mid-2015. My 95-year-old mother-in-law teetered with us till November—the biggest part of her wanting to, as she understood it, join her daughter and husband. Despite this, she was remarkable for her continuing interest in her family and their doings, volunteering how blessed she felt. There is nothing like approaching death to help focus the mind on the importance of just being with people you love. Lots of memories and stories surface, reminding of the gifts they brought by their being here.

Writing this book has been different for me—in a good way. It seems to have come from a more relaxed, sensual bit of me. Things have popped in—experiences, recollections, connections—and they popped in to a different bit of me, my body and my chest as much as my head. Lovely things have happened. Like the singer with his guitar on the 8.20 a.m. train to the city who sang his songs, including the fetchingly titled 'Facebook is Heroin', to the packed carriage—some of who remained buried in Facebook pages. When someone asked if he had a Facebook page or website so they could look up his gigs, he said he didn't and was just playing his music for people to enjoy, not to make money or become famous. I felt like cheering: mindful leadership right there on the 8.20 a.m.

Thank you to all my grown-up children—James, Amy, Huw and Charlie—for being yourselves. I love tagging along in your interests and being stretched by your respective zests for life, learning and taking on big challenges. Thank you for tolerating too many of my renditions of the Beatles and Bee Gees love songs—word for word—though I notice many are now back in favour! My grandchildren Felix, Phoebe and new Billie regularly remind me of the value of 'irrational exuberance' (so described by one of my MBS economic colleagues as they cavort down the hushed university corridors). I admit to feeling like I am regressing as I age and most at home with the youngest members of the family: a bit of porridge down my front like Phoebe and enjoying nothing better than poking around in sand, going to the movies in the middle of the day or feeding the compost worms with chicken poo. Speaking of chickens, our three newish girls—Daisy, Maisy and Ginger—have been a source of many erudite exchanges on being in the moment, though we did wonder about Daisy and her confused leadership impulses. She so often behaves like a rooster. To all my extended family—human and otherwise—thanks for the love you bring to my life.

Finally, most gratitude goes to Warwick Pattinson—companion, fellow lover of puddings and swimming—you encourage me into things not featured on the 'To do' list, things I didn't plan or necessarily think a good idea, but turn out to be so. Thanks.

ENDNOTES

Introduction
1   Kabat-Zinn (1994) *Wherever You Go, There You Are.*
2   Kabat-Zinn (2013) *Full Catastrophe Living*, p. 6.
3   Exceptions are Michael Carroll's *The Mindful Leader* (2007) and Richard Boyatzis and Annie McKee's *Resonant Leadership* (2005).
4   See Francis et al. (2012) *Seizing the Initiative*; and Damousi et al. (2014) *Diversity in Leadership: Australian women, past and present*, Australian National University e-press, Canberra, http://press.anu.edu.au/titles/diversity-in-leadership/.
5   The term 'meditations' has been used by assorted writers and philosophers, such as Descartes, to denote studying phenomena through evolving personal understandings. I use it here to capture a process of exploration that is guided by close personal attention rather than systematic intellectual analysis.

PART ONE: LEADERSHIP FOR LIFE
Chapter 1—Being as well as doing in leadership
1   Heifetz et al. (2009) *The Practice of Adaptive Leadership.*

Chapter 2—Thinking less
1   Kahneman (2011) *Thinking, Fast and Slow.*
2   Gladwell (2005) *Blink.* Also for summaries of mind-body and neural plasticity research see Norman Doidge's books *The Brain that Changes Itself* (2010) and *The Brain's Way of Healing* (2015).
3   See, for example, Kahneman and Riis (2005) 'Living and thinking about it'. On some of the dysfunctional outcomes of managerial habits of thinking see David and Congleton (2013) 'Emotional agility'.

4   For example, neuroscientist Susan Greenfield's work where the brain and mind are often conflated and brain is the seat of identity, such as *ID: The quest for identity in the 21st century* (2008), Sceptre, London.

5   Siegel (2009) *Mindsight.*

6   Hassed (2008) *The Essence of Health.*

7   I was introduced to the idea of 'excessive thinking' during meditation teacher training that I undertook at the Gawler Foundation, which drew on the work of Craig Hassed (2003, 2008, 2013), Ian Gawler (1996) and Ian Gawler and Paul Bedson (2010).

8   Gladwell in *Blink* provides several good examples of this, such as his opening case of trying to authenticate a sculpture.

9   Weick and Putnam (2006) 'Organizing for mindfulness'.

10   Vogus and Sutcliffe (2012) 'Organizational mindfulness and mindful organizing'; see also, for example, Dane (2011) 'Paying attention to mindfulness'.

11   Rock (2006) *Quiet Leadership.*

Chapter 4—Giving attention

1   See, for example, Ron Heifetz's work such as, with Linsky, *Leadership on the Line* (2002).

2   On the importance of paying attention, see Sheehan and Pearse (2014) *One Moment Please*

3   Dean and Webb (2011) *McKinsey Quarterly.*

4   Killingsworth and Gilbert (2010) 'A wandering mind'.

5   Fiol and O'Connor (2003) 'Waking up!'.

6   Kabat-Zinn (2005) *Coming to Our Senses*, p. 443.

7   ibid.

8   See https://www.ted.com/speakers/atul_gawande_1 and *Being Mortal* (2014).

9   Since 2006 I have attended four or five retreats with Rinpoche as a teacher and also read and re-read his wonderful book *The Tibetan Book of Living and Dying* (1998, 2002).

10   Adapted from Judi Marshall (1999) 'Living life as inquiry'. See also Marshall's new book entitled *First Person Action Research* (2016).

Chapter 5—Reflecting on identity with less ego

1   When I used this term with two of my sons, neither recognised it, suggesting that it is probably a dated derogatory description of being overly self-absorbed.

2   Distinctions between single, double and 'deutero' learning are explored in the work of Chris Argyris and Donald Schon, for example, *Organizational Learning: A theory of action perspective* (1978), Addison Wesley, Reading, Massachusetts.

3   This work has been informed by my two doctoral supervisors, Alan (Foo) Davies and Graham Little, who both had an interest in psycho-analysis arguing that 'leadership has a childhood'. More recently, the work of Robert Kegan and Lisa Lahey on 'big assumptions' and immunity to change brings an adult education perspective to the value of reflection on histories. See, for example, *How the Way We Talk Can Change the Way We Work* (2001), Jossey Bass, San Francisco and *Immunity to Change* (2009), Harvard Business School Press, Boston, Massachusetts.

4   Crucibles are 'intense transformative experiences'. For more on their role in leadership, see W. Bennis and R. Thomas (2002) 'Crucibles of leadership', *Harvard Business Review*; Bennis and Thomas (2002) *Geeks and Geezers: How era, values and defining moments change leadership*, Harvard Business School Press, Boston, Massachusetts; and A. Sinclair and V. Wilson (2002) *New Faces of Leadership*, Carlton South, Melbourne University Press.

5   For useful discussions of concepts of ego, self and identity in both Buddhist and therapeutic traditions, see Aronson (2004) *Buddhist Practice on Eastern Ground* and Rubin (1996) *Psychotherapy and Buddhism*.

6   For more on this critique of authentic leadership, see my chapter 'Can I really be me?' in Ladkin and Spiller (2013) *Authentic Leadership*.

7   Kahane (2010) *Power and Love*, p. 136.

Chapter 6—Listening from stillness

1   See, for example, Searle (2011) 'Could it be as simple as listening?'.

2   In, for example, *You are Here: Discovering the magic of the present moment* (2012).

3   Miriam Rose Ungunmerr-Baumann of the Ngangikurungkurr people in the Daly River area of the Australian Northern Territory is a recognised elder spokesperson on dadirri practices. See https://www.youtube.com/watch?v=pkY1dGk-LyE.

Chapter 7—Dialogue for insight

1   Kramer (2007) *Insight Dialogue*.

2   Isaacs (1999) *Dialogue and the Art of Thinking Together*, p. 255.

Chapter 8—Connecting

1   Kets de Vries (2014) *Mindful Leadership Coaching*, p. 197.

2   ibid., p. 175.

3   ibid., p. 184.

4   Year-round mindfulness training is available outside of the May campaign at the Mind Life Project (www.mindlifeproject.com).

Chapter 9—Being mindful in crises
1   Atkins (2008) 'Leadership as response not reaction'.
2   Weick and Putnam (2006) 'Organizing for mindfulness'.
3   Weick et al. (1999) 'Organizing for high reliability'.
4   See Charles Perrow (1984) *Normal Accidents*, Basic Books, New York.
5   Fiol and O'Connor (2003) 'Waking up!'.
6   Paul t'Hart (2014) *Understanding Public Management*; see also Boin et al. (2005) *The Politics of Crisis Management: Public leadership under pressure*, Cambridge University Press, Cambridge.

Chapter 10—Transforming writing
1   Helen Sword (2012) *Stylish Academic Writing*, Harvard University Press, Cambridge, Massachusetts.
2   Don Watson (2003) *Death Sentence: The decay of public language*, Knopf, Milsons Point, NSW.
3   See Michel de Montaigne (1958 trans. J. Cohen) *Essays*, Penguin Books, Harmondsworth, Middlesex, and for a highly readable summary see also Sarah Bakewell (2010) *How to Live: Or, a life of Montaigne in one question and twenty attempts at an answer*, Chatto and Windus, London.
4   ibid., p. 11.
5   Bakewell, op.cit.

PART TWO: LEADING WITH BODY
1   Hanh (2013) *Peace of Mind*.
2   See, for example, Senge et al. (2004) *Presence*.
3   Ladkin (2010) *Rethinking Leadership*.

Chapter 11—Breathing consciously
1   Swami Rama (1978) *Science of Breath: A practical guide*, R. Ballentine and A. Hymes, Himalayan Institute Press, Honesdale, Pennsylvania.
2   Hanh (1996) *Breathe! You are alive*, p. 5.
3   Hanh (1991) *The Miracle of Mindfulness*, p. 4.
4   ibid., p. 15.
5   The metaphor of infancy may be apt as often people are encouraged to learn 'belly breathing' from babies.
6   Undertaken at Antioch University, I was lucky enough to be the external reader for this dissertation.
7   Ladkin (2014) 'In through the nose, out through the mouth'.
8   ibid., p. 235.

Chapter 12—Looking after bodies

1   Gladwell (2005) *Blink*.
2   See Sinclair (2013) 'Can I really be me?'.
3   See, for example, 'Body possibilities in leadership' (2005) and *Leadership for the Disillusioned* (2007).
4   Ciulla (2010) 'Being there'.
5   For a more extended discussion, see Sinclair (2005 and 2007).
6   I describe some of these experiences in more detail in Amanda Sinclair (2005) 'Body and management pedagogy', *Gender Work and Organization*, 12(1), pp. 89–104.

Chapter 13—Tuning into the senses

1   Kabat-Zinn (2005) *Coming to our senses*, p. 166.
2   See also a critique of conventional notions of 'sense-making' which privilege cognitive over embodied processes in Ann Cunliffe and Chris Coupland (2012).
3   Kathleen Riach and Samantha Warren (2015) 'Smell organization: Bodies and corporeal porosity in office work', *Human Relations*, 68(5), pp. 789–809.
4   Interest in the senses is occurring in organisation studies and management; see, for example, Riach and Warren ibid., and more broadly in anthropology and social theory see, for example, D. Howes (2010) *Sensual Relations: Engaging the senses in culture and social theory*, University of Michigan Press, Ann Arbor, Michigan.
5   See, for example, John Paul Stephens, 'Leading through feeling', one of a number of interesting chapters on learning from musical leadership in Donna Ladkin and Steve Taylor's *The Physicality of Leadership* (2014), Emerald Group, Bingley, UK.
6   Stone et al.'s *Difficult Conversations* (2000) provides useful insights and strategies for working with emotion.
7   I learned about this distinction from Paul Bedson and his work at the Gawler Foundation.

Chapter 14—Finding pleasure

1   *Teaching to Transgress: Education as the practice of freedom* (1994), Routledge, New York.
2   *Pedagogical Pleasures* (1999), Peter Lang Publishing, New York, p. 16; see also bell hooks, ibid.
3   Luce Irigaray (2002) *The Way of Love*, Continuum, London.
4   Julie Laible (2003) 'A loving epistemology: What I hold critical in my life, faith and profession' in M. Young and L. Skrla (eds) *Reconsidering*

Feminist Research in Educational Leadership, State University of New York Press, Albany, New York, pp. 179–192.

5   See Bell and Sinclair (2014).
6   Epstein (2005) *Open to Desire.*
7   ibid., p. 14

Chapter 15—Opening to creativity

1   Jill Bolte Taylor (2008) *My Stroke of Insight: A brain scientist's personal journey,* Viking, New York; see also her TED talk, http://www.ted.com/talks/jill_bolte_taylor_s_powerful_stroke_of_insight?language=en.
2   A. Morin (2009) 'Self-awareness deficits following loss of inner speech: Dr. Jill Bolte Taylor's case study', *Consciousness and Cognition*, 18(2), pp. 524–529.
3   Palmo (2011) *Into the Heart of Life*, p. 172.
4   For an exploration of research about intuition and 'fast' thinking, see Gladwell's *Blink* (2005) and Kahneman's *Thinking, Fast and Slow* (2011) that were also discussed in Chapter 2.
5   Interview on ABC Radio National 'Arts Today', 16 March 2015.
6   In 2012 the Bendigo Art Gallery attracted 314,000 visitors, more than half the other Victorian regional galleries combined. In 100 days in 2012 it brought in $16 million in tourism revenue to Bendigo.

PART THREE: LEADING WITH HEART

1   For an exploration of examples of leading with heart, see Steve Taylor's 'Open your heart' (2014).
2   See, for example, research from the Center for Compassion and Altruism Research and Education, Stanford University, ccare.stanford.edu; and the work of James Doty, described on pp. 17–20 in Thupten Jinpa (2015) *A Fearless Heart*; also the work of Barbara Fredrickson and colleagues on the impact of loving kindness meditation (2008) 'Open hearts build lives'.

Chapter 16—Feeling

1   The approach described here was just part of a wide-ranging set of initiatives. For a more comprehensive description of actions to reform the police and community response to family violence, see the Australian and New Zealand School of Government (ANZSOG) case study (2009) 'Victoria Police and family violence', www.casestudies.anzsog.edu.au.
2   See Jinpa (2005) *A Fearless Heart* for a description of the program and the research; also ccare.stanford.edu.
3   A. Hochschild (1983) *The Managed Heart: The commercialization of human feelings*, University of California Press, Berkeley, California.

Chapter 17—Being ourselves?

1 On women being subject to pressures to camouflage themselves in order to do leadership see, for example, Sinclair (1998) *Doing Leadership Differently*; A. Eagly and L. Carli (2007) *Through the Labyrinth: The truth about how women become leaders*, Harvard Business School Press, Boston, Massachusetts.

2 For more on authenticity and women in leadership, see Sinclair (2013) 'Can I really be me?'.

3 For more critical views on authenticity, see Ladkin and Spiller (2013) *Authentic Leadership*.

4 Jo Brewis (2004) 'Refusing to be "me"' in R. Thomas, A. Mills and J. Helms Mills (eds), *Identity Politics at Work*, Routledge, London, p. 29.

5 See Rubin (1996) and Aronson (2004) for explorations of different ways Western psychology, psychoanalysis and Buddhism sees the self, and differences in the remedies prescribed for reducing individual suffering.

Chapter 18—Clarifying purpose, going for happiness

1 'A simple practice for all people everywhere' by His Holiness the Dalai Lama, distributed by the Tara Institute, Brighton, Victoria (www.tara institute.com.au).

2 See my book chapter 'Leading with Body' (2011) in Emma Jeanes, David Knights and Patricia Yancey Martin (eds), *Handbook of Gender, Work and Organization*, John Wiley and Sons, Chichester, UK, pp. 117–130, which begins with a media story about Cameron Clyne, former CEO of National Australia Bank, and his swimming prowess as evidence of leadership capability.

3 Champions of Change are a group of senior Australian business leaders brought together by Sex Discrimination Commissioner Elizabeth Broderick, and who share a view that it is the responsibility of male leaders to lead change on gender equality.

4 This research was subsequently written up by Valerie and I in *New Faces of Leadership* (2002), Melbourne University Press, Carlton South.

5 This description of Gordon's philosophy and actions come from my knowledge and research of his leadership, his comments at the Mindful Leadership Global Forum, Sydney in 2014 and a conferring address to a Sydney University graduation in 2014.

Chapter 19—Being ethical

1 R. Lisle Baker and Daniel Brown (2014) 'On engagement: Learning to pay attention', *UALR Law Review*, 36, pp. 337–338.

2 Ladkin (2015) *Mastering the Ethical Dimensions of Organizations*.

3 For critiques of corporate uses of mindfulness, see Purser and Loy (2013) 'Beyond McMindfulness', and R. Purser and J. Milillo (2014) 'Corporate mindfulness is bullsh*t', salon.com, 28 September 2015.

4   Hanh (2009) *You are Here*
5   Confino (2013) 'Thich Nhat, Hanh'.

Chapter 20—Bringing love and compassion into leadership

1   Melbourne Football Club are known as the Demons, whose motto is 'My heart beats true'.
2   Paul and Tami Roos were speakers at the Global Forum in Mindful Leadership held in Sydney, 2014 and organised by the Wake-up Foundation. See also Lucille Keen 'Paul Roos' secret for AFL success: Meditation' in *Australian Financial Review*'s *Boss Magazine*, 11 July 2014, and Tami Roos' book *The Gift: Presence to power*, www.tamiroos.com.
3   For an elegant and readable account of Goethe's views on love as central to life, see John Armstrong's *Love, Life, Goethe: How to be happy in an imperfect world* (2006) Allen Lane, London.
4   See the work of Bruce Perry, for example, B. Perry and E. Hambrick (2008) 'The neurosequential model of therapeutics', *Reclaiming Children and Youth*, 17(3), pp. 38–43.
5   Mirror neurons were first identified in monkeys by Italian researchers Giacomo Rizzolatti and his collegues at the University of Parma. Since then they have enjoyed great attention for what they tell us about the role of empathy in humans. For an engaging presentation on mirror neurons see the TED talk by V. S. Ramachandran, http://www.ted.com/talks/vs_ramachandran_the_neurons_that_shaped_civilization?language=en.
6   His Holiness the Dalai Lama and Van den Muyzenberg (2008) *The Leader's Way*, p. 67.
7   Klein (2014) *This Changes Everything*, p. 342.
8   Joanna Macy (2007) *World as Lover, World as Self*; see also her (2014) *Coming Back to Life: Practices to reconnect our lives, our world*, New Society Publishers, New York.
9   Steve Taylor (2014) 'Open your heart' in Donna Ladkin and Steve Taylor (eds), *The Physicality of Leadership*, Emerald Group, Bingley, UK, p. 240.
10 On the exploration of these 'big assumptions', see the work of adult educationalists Robert Kegan and Lisa Lahey, *How the Way we Talk can Change the Way we Work* (2002), Jossey-Bass, San Francisco and *Immunity to Change* (2009), Harvard Business Review Press, Boston, Massachusetts.
11 tibetoffice.org website, http://tibetoffice.org/media-press/news/the-dalai-lama-speaks-to-15000-people-in-mexico-city-on-secular-ethics, accessed 13 May 2015.
12 Buddhist teacher Philippa Ransome introduced me to the extensive writings and teaching of Ayya Khema, for many of which she is custodian.

FURTHER READING ON
MINDFULNESS AND LEADERSHIP

Aronson, H. (2004) *Buddhist Practice on Western Ground: Reconciling eastern ideals and western psychology*. Boston, Massachusetts: Shambhala Publications.

Atkins, P. (2008) 'Leadership as response not reaction: Wisdom and mindfulness in public sector leadership' in t' Hart, P. and Uhr, J. *Public Leadership: Perspectives and practices*. Canberra: ANU Press.

Atkinson, J. (2002) *Trauma Trails Recreating Song Lines: The transgenerational effect of trauma in Indigenous Australians*. North Melbourne: Spinifex Press.

Bell, E. and Sinclair, A. (2014) 'Reclaiming eroticism in the academy', *Organization*, 21(2): 268–280.

Boin, A. and t' Hart, P. (2010) 'Organizing for effective crisis management: Lessons from research', *Australian Journal of Public Administration*, 69(4): 357–371.

Boyatzis, R. and McKee, A. (2005) *Resonant Leadership: Renewing yourself and connecting with others through mindfulness, hope and compassion*. Boston, Massachusetts: Harvard Business School Press.

Brown, K. W. and Ryan, R. M. (2003) 'The benefits of being present: Mindfulness and its role in psychological well-being', *Journal of Personality and Social Psychology*, 84(4): 822.

Brown, K. W., Ryan, R. M., et al. (2007) 'Mindfulness: Theoretical foundations and evidence for its salutary effects', *Psychological Inquiry*, 18(4): 211–237.

Carroll, M. (2007). *The Mindful Leader: Ten principles for bringing out the best in ourselves and others*. Boston, Massachusetts: Trumpeter.

Ciulla, J. (2010) 'Being there: Why leaders should not "fiddle" while Rome burns', *Presidential Studies Quarterly*, 40(1): 38–56.

Confino, J. (2013) 'Thich Nhat Hanh: Is mindfulness being corrupted by business and finance?' the guardian.com.

Cunliffe, A. and Coupland, C. (2012) 'From hero to villain to hero: Making experiences sensible through embodied narrative sense-making', *Human Relations*, 65(1): 63–88.

Dane, E. (2011) 'Paying attention to mindfulness and its effect on task performance in the workplace', *Journal of Management*, 37(4): 997–1018.

David, S. and Congleton, C. (2013) 'Emotional agility: How effective leaders manage their thoughts and feelings', *Harvard Business Review*, November: 125.

Davidson, R., Kabat-Zinn, J. et al. (2003) 'Alterations in brain and immune function produced by mindfulness meditation', *Psychosomatic Medicine*, 65: 564–570.

Dean, D. and Webb, C. (2011) 'Recovering from information overload', *McKinsey Quarterly*, January.

Doidge, N. (2010) *The Brain that Changes Itself: Stories of personal triumph from the frontiers of brain science*. North Carlton, Victoria: Scribe.

Doidge, N. (2015) *The Brain's Way of Healing: Remarkable discoveries and recoveries from the frontiers of neuroplasticity*. Brunswick, Victoria: Scribe.

Epstein, M. (2005) *Open to Desire: The truth about what the Buddha taught*. New York: Penguin/Gotham Books.

Fiol, C. and O'Connor, E. (2003) 'Waking up! Mindfulness in the face of bandwagons', *Academy of Management Review*, 28(1): 54–70.

Francis, R., Grimshaw, P. and Standish, A. (2012) *Seizing the Initiative: Australian women leaders in politics, workplaces and communities*. Melbourne University e-press.

Fredrickson, B. L., Cohn, M. A., Coffey, K. A., Pek, J. and Finkel, S. M. (2008) 'Open hearts build lives: Positive emotions, induced through loving-kindness meditation, build consequential personal resources', *Journal of Personality and Social Psychology*, 95(5), 1045–1062.

Gawande, A. (2014) *Being Mortal: Illness, medicine and what really matters in the end*. London: Profile Books.

Gawler, I. (1996) *Meditation: Pure and simple*. South Yarra, Victoria: Michelle Anderson Publishing.

Gawler, I. and Bedson, P. (2010) *Meditation: An in-depth guide*. Crows Nest, NSW: Allen & Unwin.

Gladwell, M. (2005) *Blink: The power of thinking without thinking*. London: Allen Lane.

Goleman, D. (2003) (ed.) *Healing Emotions: Conversations with the Dalai Lama on mindfulness, emotions and health*. Boston, Massachusetts: Shambhala Publications.

Hanh, T. N. (1991) *The Miracle of Mindfulness: A manual on meditation*. London: Rider.

Hanh, T. N. (1996) *Breathe! You are Alive: Sutra on the full awareness of breathing*. Berkeley, California: Parallax Press.

Hanh, T. N. (2003) *Creating True Peace: Ending violence in yourself, your family, your community and the world*. New York: Free Press.

Hanh, T. N. (2006 trans. Sherab Chödzin Kohn) *True Love: A practice for awakening the heart*. Boston, Massachusetts: Shambhala Publications.

Hanh, T. N. (2012) *You are Here: Discovering the magic of the present moment*. Boston, Massachusetts: Shambhala Publications.

Hanh, T. N. (2013) *Peace of Mind: Becoming fully present*. Berkeley, California: Parallax Press.

Hassed, C. (2003) *Know Thyself: The stress release programme*. Melbourne: Michelle Anderson Publishing.

Hassed, C. (2008) *The Essence of Health: The seven pillars of wellbeing*. North Sydney: Ebury Press, Random House.

Hassed, C. (2013) 'Driven to distraction: Why be mindful in this unmindful world?' in Blashki, G. and Sykes, H. (eds) *Life Surfing Life Dancing*, Sydney: Future Leaders, pp. 43–66.

Hassed, C. and Chambers, R. (2014) *Mindful Learning: Reduce stress and improve brain performance for learning*. Woolombi, NSW: Exisle Publishing.

Heifetz, R. A. (1995) *Leadership Without Easy Answers*. Cambridge, Massachusetts: Belknap Press of Harvard University Press.

Heifetz, R. A. and Linsky, M. (2002). 'A survival guide for leaders', *Harvard Business Review*, 80(6): 65–74.

Heifetz, R. and Linsky, M. (2002) *Leadership on the Line: Staying alive through the dangers of leading*. Boston, Massachusetts: Harvard Business School Publishing.

Heifetz, R., Grashow, A. and Linsky, M. (2009) *The Practice of Adaptive Leadership: Tools and tactics for changing your organisation and the world*. Boston, Massachusetts: Harvard Business School Publishing.

His Holiness the Dalai Lama (2003) *Lighting the Path*. South Melbourne: Lothian.

His Holiness the Dalai Lama and Van den Muyzenberg, L. (2008) *The Leader's Way*. London: Nicholas Brearley.

Hölzel, B. K., Carmody, J. et al. (2011) 'Mindfulness practice leads to increases in regional brain gray matter density', *Psychiatry Research*, 19(1): 36–43.

Hölzel, B. K., Lazar, S. W. et al. (2011) 'How does mindfulness meditation work? Proposing mechanisms of action from a conceptual and neural perspective', *Perspectives on Psychological Science*, 6(6): 537–559.

Isaacs, W. (1999) *Dialogue and the Art of Thinking Together*. New York: Random House Inc.

Jinpa, T. (2015) *A Fearless Heart: Why compassion is the key to greater well-being*. London: Piatkus.

Kabat-Zinn, J. (1994) *Wherever You Go, There You Are: Mindfulness meditation in everyday life*. New York: Hyperion.

Kabat-Zinn, J. (2005) *Coming to Our Senses: Healing ourselves and the world through mindfulness*. New York: Hyperion.

Kabat-Zinn, J. (2013, 2nd edn) *Full Catastrophe Living: Using the wisdom of your mind to face stress, pain and illness*. New York: Bantam.

Kahane, A. (2010) *Power and Love: A theory and practice of social change*. San Francisco: Berrett-Koehler.

Kahneman, D. and Riis, J. (2005) 'Living and thinking about it: Two perspectives on life' in Huppert, F., Baylis, N. et al. (eds) *The Science of Well-Being*. Oxford: Oxford University Press, pp. 185–304.

Kahneman, D. (2011) *Thinking, Fast and Slow*. Camberwell, Victoria: Allen Lane.

Kets de Vries, M. F. (2014) *Mindful Leadership Coaching: Journeys into the interior*. Basingstoke: Palgrave Macmillan.

Khema, A. (1987) *Being Nobody, Going Nowhere: Meditations on the Buddhist path*. Boston, Massachusetts: Wisdom Publications.

Killingsworth, M. and Gilbert, T. (2010) 'A wandering mind is an unhappy mind', *Science*, 330: 932 DOI: 10.1126/science.1192439.

Klein, N. (2014) *This Changes Everything: Capitalism vs the climate*. New York: Simon & Schuster.

Kok, B. and Fredrickson, B. (2010) 'Upward spirals of the heart: Autonomic flexibility, as indexed by vagal tone, reciprocally and prospectively predicts positive emotions and social connectedness', *Biological Psychology*, 85(3): 432–436.

Kramer, G. (2007) *Insight Dialogue: The interpersonal path to freedom*. Boston, Massachusetts: Shambhala Publications.

Ladkin, D. (2008) 'Leading beautifully: How mastery, congruence and purpose create the aesthetic of embodied leadership practice', *The Leadership Quarterly*, 19: 31–41.

Ladkin, D. (2010) *Rethinking Leadership: A new look at old leadership questions*. Cheltenham, UK: Edward Elgar.

Ladkin, D. and Spiller, C. (eds) (2013) *Authentic Leadership: Clashes, convergences and coalescences*. Cheltenham, UK; Northampton, Massachusetts: Edward Elgar.

Ladkin, D. (2014) 'In through the nose, out through the mouth: How conscious breathing can help mere mortals cope with the difficulties of leading' in Ladkin, D. and Taylor, S. (eds) *The Physicality of Leadership: Gesture, entanglement, taboo, possibilities.* Bingley, UK: Emerald Group, pp. 221–237.

Ladkin, D. (2015) *Mastering the Ethical Dimensions of Organizations: A self-reflective guide to developing ethical astuteness.* Cheltenham, UK: Edward Elgar.

Langer, E. J. (1989) 'Minding matters: The consequences of mindlessness-mindfulness', *Advances in Experimental Social Psychology*, 22: 137–173.

Langer, E. J. (1992). 'Matters of mind: Mindfulness/mindlessness in perspective', *Consciousness and Cognition*, 1(3): 289–305.

Lazar, S., Kerr, C. et al. (2005) 'Meditation experience is associated with increased cortical thickness', *Neuroreport*, 16(17): 1893–1897.

Macy, J. (2007) *World as Lover, World as Self: Courage for global justice and ecological renewal.* Berkeley, California: Parallax Press.

Marshall, J. (1999) 'Living life as inquiry', *Systemic Practice and Action Research*, 12(2): 155–171.

Marshall, J. (2016) *First Person Action Research: Living life as inquiry.* London: Sage Publications.

McCormick, D. and Hunter, J. (2008) 'Mindfulness in the workplace: An exploratory study', paper presented at the 2008 Academy of Management Annual Meeting, Annaheim, California.

Palmo, T. (2011) *Into the Heart of Life: Buddhist teachings on wisdom and compassion.* Crows Nest, NSW: Allen & Unwin.

Purser, R. and Loy, D. (2013) 'Beyond McMindfulness', *Huffington Post*, huffingtonpost.com, posted 2 July 2013.

Purser, R. E. and Milillo, J. (2014) 'Mindfulness revisited: A Buddhist-based conceptualization', *Journal of Management Inquiry*: 1056492614532315.

Queen, C. and King, S. (eds) (1996) *Engaged Buddhism: Buddhist liberation movements in Asia.* Albany: State University of New York Press.

Reudy, N. and Schweitzer, M. (2010) 'In the moment: The effect of mindfulness on ethical decision-making', *Journal of Business Ethics*, 95(1): 73–87.

Ricard, M. (2008 trans. Sherab Chödzin Kohn) *The Art of Meditation.* London: Atlantic Books.

Rinpoche, S. (2002) *The Tibetan Book of Living and Dying* (revised edn). New York: HarperCollins.

Rock, D. (2006) *Quiet Leadership.* New York: HarperCollins.

Roos, T. (2012) *The Gift: Presence to power.* Createspace. http://www.tamiroos.com/books.

Rubin, J. (1996) *Psychotherapy and Buddhism: Toward an integration.* New York: Plenum Press.

Scharmer, C. O. (2009) *Theory U: Learning from the future as it emerges.* San Francisco: Berrett-Koehler Publishers.

Salzberg, S. and Kabat-Zinn, J. (1997, 2003) 'Mindfulness as medicine' in Goleman, D. (ed.) *Healing Emotions: Conversations with the Dalai Lama on mindfulness, emotions and health.* Boston, Massachusetts: Shambhala Publications, pp. 107–144.

Searle, R. (2011). 'Could it be as simple as listening?', www.searleburke.com.

Searle, R. (2013). 'Seven elements of insight dialogue', www.searleburke.com.

Senge, P. M., Scharmer, C. O. et al. (2004) *Presence: Human purpose and the field of the future.* Cambridge, Massachusetts: Society of Organizational Learning Inc.

Shapiro, S. L., Astin, J., Bishop, S. and Cordova, M. (2005) 'Mindfulness-based stress reduction for health care professionals: Results from a randomized trial', *International Journal of Stress Management,* 12(2): 164–176.

Shapiro, S.L., Carlson, L. E. et al. (2006) 'Mechanisms of mindfulness', *Journal of Clinical Psychology,* 62(3): 373–386.

Shapiro, S., Oman, D., Thoresen, C., Plante, T. and Flinders, T. (2008) 'Cultivating mindfulness: Effects on well-being', *Journal of Clinical Psychology,* 64(7): 840–862.

Sheehan, M. and Pearse, S. (2015) *One Moment Please: It's time to pay attention.* California: Hay House.

Siegel, D. (2009) *Mindsight: Change your brain and your life.* Melbourne: Scribe.

Sinclair, A. (1998, 2005) *Doing Leadership Differently: Gender, power and sexuality in a changing business culture.* Carlton South, Victoria: Melbourne University Press.

Sinclair, A. (2004) 'Renewal', *Mt Eliza Business Review,* 7(1): 38–44.

Sinclair, A. (2005) 'Body possibilities in leadership', *Leadership,* 1(4): 387–406.

Sinclair, A. (2007) *Leadership for the Disillusioned: Moving beyond myths and heroes to leading that liberates.* Crows Nest, NSW: Allen & Unwin.

Sinclair, A. (2013) 'Can I really be me? The challenges for women leaders constructing authenticity' in Ladkin, D. and Spiller, C. *Authentic Leadership: Clashes, convergences and coalescences.* Cheltenham, UK; Northampton, Massachusetts: Edward Elgar, pp. 239–251.

Sinclair, A. (2015) 'Possibilities, purpose and pitfalls: Insights from introducing mindfulness to leaders', *Journal of Spirituality, Leadership and Management,* 8(1): 3–11, http://dx.doi.org/10.15183/slm2015.08.1112; http://www.slam.org.au/publications/journal/volume-8-2015/.

Stone, D., Patton, B. and Heen, S. (2000) *Difficult Conversations: How to discuss what matters most.* New York: Penguin Books.

Taylor, S. (2014) 'Open your heart' in Ladkin, D. and Taylor, S. (eds) *The Physicality of Leadership: Gesture, entanglement, taboo, possibilities.* Bingley, UK: Emerald Group, pp. 239–252.

t' Hart, P. (2014) *Understanding Public Management*. London: Palgrave Macmillan.

Trungpa, C. (1973) *Cutting Through Spiritual Materialism*. Boston, Massachusetts: Shambhala Publications.

van den Hurk, P. A., Giommi, F. et al. (2010) 'Greater efficiency in attentional processing related to mindfulness meditation', *The Quarterly Journal of Experimental Psychology*, 3(6): 1168–1180.

van den Hurk, P. A., Janssen, B. H. et al. (2010) 'Mindfulness meditation associated with alterations in bottom-up processing: Psychophysiological evidence for reduced reactivity', *International Journal of Psychophysiology*, 78(2): 151–157.

Varela, F., Thompson, E. and Rosch, E. (1993) *The Embodied Mind: Cognitive science and human experience*. Cambridge, Massachusetts: MIT Press.

Vogus, T. and Sutcliffe, E. (2012) 'Organizational mindfulness and mindful organizing: A reconceptualization and path forward', *Academy of Management Learning and Education*, 11(4): 722–735.

Wallace, B. Alan (2006) *The Attention Revolution: Unlocking the power of the focused mind*. Somerville, Massachusetts: Wisdom Publications.

Wallace, B. Alan and Shapiro, S. (2006) 'Mental balance and well-being: Building bridges between Buddhism and Western psychology', *American Psychologist*, 161(7): 690–701.

Weick, K., Sutcliffe, K. and Obstfeld, D. (1999) 'Organizing for high reliability: Processes of collective mindfulness' in Staw, B. and Sutton, R. (eds) *Research in Organizational Behavior* vol. 21. Greenwich, Connecticut: JAI Press, pp. 81–123.

Weick, K. and Putnam, T. (2006) 'Organizing for mindfulness: Eastern wisdom and Western knowledge', *Journal of Management Inquiry*, 15(3): 275–287.

Weick, K. and Sutcliffe, K. (2006) 'Mindfulness and the quality of organizational attention', *Organization Science*, 17(4): 514–525.

INDEX